KT-498-765

MONTY ROBERTS

THE HORSES IN MY LIFE

headline

*I dedicate this book to my grandchildren, Matthew and Adam Loucks;
and Loren Frances Roberts, daughter of son, Marty, and Heather Roberts.
This is a part of your heritage. And I can't leave out our extended family,
the foster children who have also enriched our lives. I hope all of you enjoy
reading the special stories about 'The Horses in My Life'.*

Copyright © 2004 Monty Roberts and Pat Roberts

The right of Monty Roberts to be identified as the Author of
the Work has been asserted by him in accordance with the
Copyright, Designs and Patents Act 1988.

First published in 2004
by HEADLINE BOOK PUBLISHING

10 9 8 7 6 5 4 3

Apart from any use permitted under UK copyright law, this publication may only
be reproduced, stored, or transmitted, in any form, or by any means, with prior
permission in writing of the publishers or, in the case of reprographic production,
in accordance with the terms of licences issued by the Copyright Licensing
Agency.

Every effort has been made to fulfil requirements with regard to reproducing
copyright material. The author and publisher will be glad to rectify any omissions
at the earliest opportunity.

A CIP catalogue record for this title is available from the British Library

ISBN 0 7553 1343 7

Design by Isobel Gillan
Printed and bound in France by Imprimerie Pollina-n°L94992

Headline's policy is to use papers that are natural, renewable and recyclable
products and made from wood grown in sustainable forests. The logging and
manufacturing processes are expected to conform to the environmental
regulations of the country of origin.

HEADLINE BOOK PUBLISHING
A division of Hodder Headline
338 Euston Road
London NW1 3BH

www.headline.co.uk
www.hodderheadline.com

ENDPAPERS © David Stoecklein/CORBIS
TITLE PAGE PHOTOGRAPH *Monty and Johnny Tivio at a cutting competition,
Tucson, 1966*

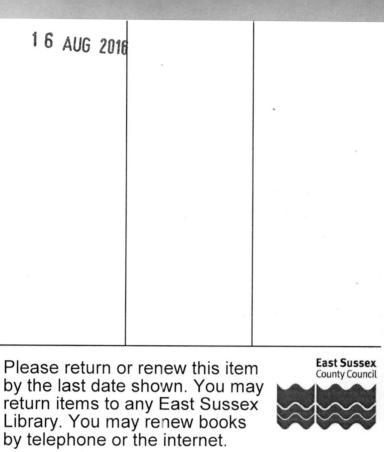

16 AUG 2016

Please return or renew this item by the last date shown. You may return items to any East Sussex Library. You may renew books by telephone or the internet.

East Sussex
County Council

0345 60 80 195 for renewals
0345 60 80 196 for enquiries

Library and Information Services
eastsussex.gov.uk/libraries

04157647 - **ITEM**

CONTENTS

NECKLACE
WITHOUT HORSES

A LEATHER STRIP –
NO BEGINNING AND
NO END

RATHER LIKE THE CIRCLE OF
LIFE WITH NO PURPOSE

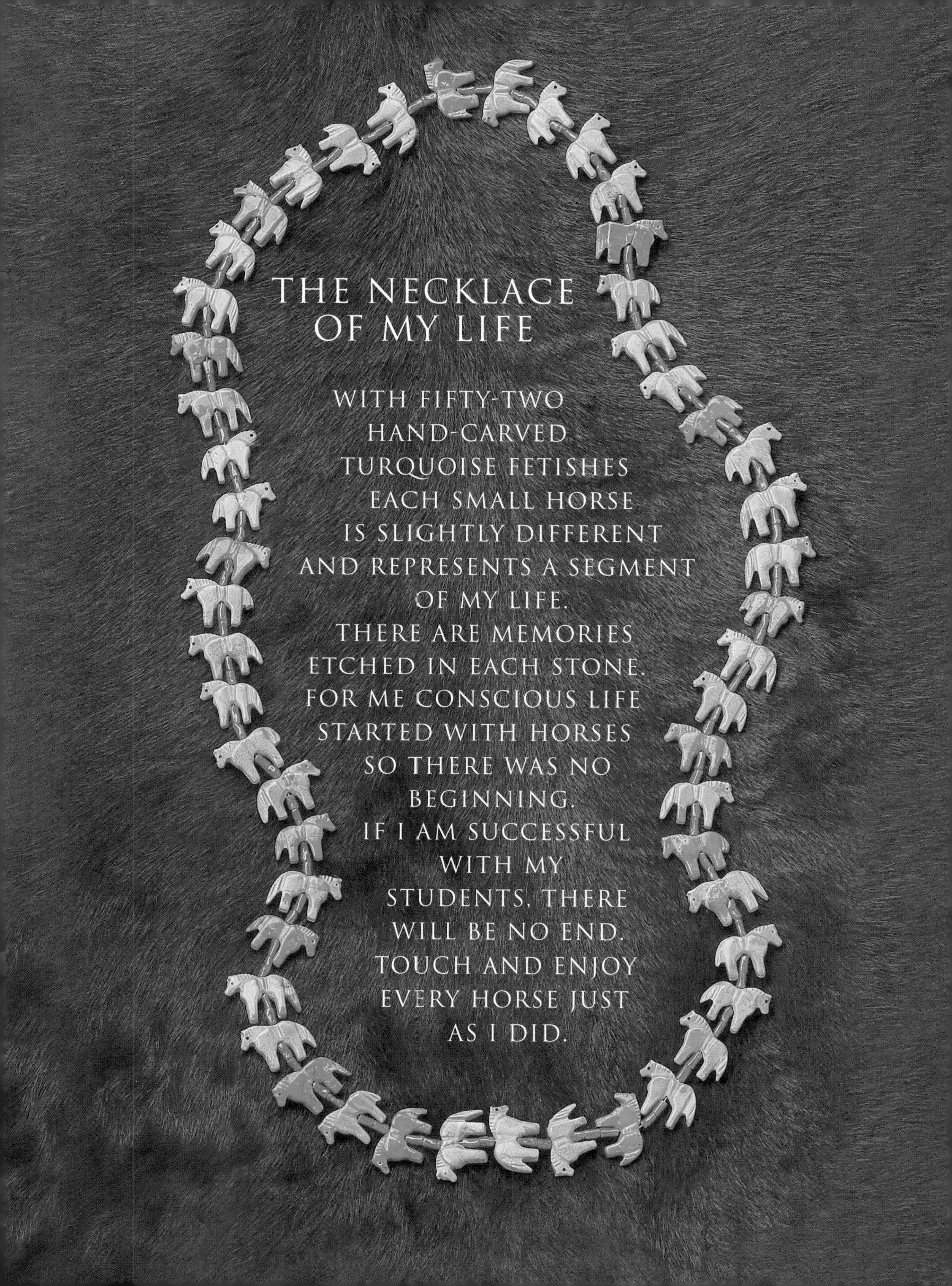

THE NECKLACE OF MY LIFE

WITH FIFTY-TWO
HAND-CARVED
TURQUOISE FETISHES
EACH SMALL HORSE
IS SLIGHTLY DIFFERENT
AND REPRESENTS A SEGMENT
OF MY LIFE.
THERE ARE MEMORIES
ETCHED IN EACH STONE.
FOR ME CONSCIOUS LIFE
STARTED WITH HORSES
SO THERE WAS NO
BEGINNING.
IF I AM SUCCESSFUL
WITH MY
STUDENTS, THERE
WILL BE NO END.
TOUCH AND ENJOY
EVERY HORSE JUST
AS I DID.

INTRODUCTION

In the early 1990s, at the suggestion of Her Majesty, Queen Elizabeth, my wife Pat and I began to write down memories of what had happened in our lives in order to tell the world about my non-violent training methods. The result was an autobiography, *The Man Who Listens to Horses*, which jumped on to the bestseller lists of about ten countries, remaining on the *New York Times* list for fifty-eight weeks.

Unlike most authors, I was able to meet my readers at public demonstrations of my techniques and I have now personally shown well over a million people that it is not necessary, and in fact positively counter-productive, to use violence in training horses. While conducting these demonstrations, I often find myself talking about the horses that have meant so much to me throughout my life. No one else has had the opportunity to deal with horses from such a wide variety of disciplines as I have – racing, show-jumping, dressage, rodeo, pleasure and trail horses and Western competition are just a few of the categories. I began to think the horses needed a book of their own.

It was an exciting prospect but little did I know how much joy I would derive from delving deep in my memory to describe these wonderful members of our extended family.

The horses that grace these pages are not necessarily all champions but they have all affected my life in a profound manner. Horses with limited talent

Lomitas

were still, and will continue to be, my teachers. It is my pledge to live the rest of my life in an attempt not to disappoint any of them.

There are sad memories, for sure, but most are happy ones. You don't have to be a professional trainer to have your life changed by a horse. Every child who has been associated with a horse is likely to cherish memories of the wonderful times they spent together. Those children and the adults they grow to be already know that it's OK to love your horse. It would be wonderful if I could bring the world to realize that to force and dominate is simply not necessary, but it is quite appropriate, and more effective, to love and appreciate.

During the writing of this book, one of my main concerns was deciding which horses to include. As I pondered this question, a certain theme kept winding its way through my brain. For some reason – perhaps it had something to do with my Cherokee heritage – I constantly returned to thoughts of a necklace. My ancestors considered a necklace to be the circle of life, and the beads or stones that hung from it were the circumstances that indelibly affected life. Now, as I travel the world, I find that native people everywhere have a similar tradition involving a necklace. The North American Indians often carve stone in the image of animals. These are generally referred to as fetishes. Across the equator, the south-sea islanders use jade-like stones carved to depict their life and to identify tribes and clans. The Arctic people use the carved tusks of sea creatures, while Africans often use bones.

I kept seeing a long, circular string with no knot, no beginning and no end. As I mentally examined the string, which was probably fashioned from the hide of a buffalo or bull elk, I came to the conclusion that it was unbreakable. I remembered Ginger. I had been riding him before my memory kicked in, so my life with horses had no beginning. It simply appeared from the fog of infancy. I survived a difficult childhood by travelling on the backs of horses and, in adulthood, the pattern didn't change. Each significant horse was a stone in my life's necklace. I used the lessons they taught me and gained strength from the relationships formed with them. I grasped each stone of my necklace, searching for the lesson it brought that was critical to my survival.

Of course, I had to include my first horse, and those of international importance. The world champions and the ones the public have come to associate with me are essential elements of my life's necklace. While fame and fortune constitute reasons for inclusion, so too do the experiences provided by wonderful horses that were never famous but enriched my life. I may never have survived without the silent contributions of these unsung heroes.

With time to reflect on this idea of each horse being a stone in my necklace of life, I came to the conclusion that the rule I should follow was that if a horse was left out and it created a gap, causing the necklace to fall apart, the horse should remain. Conversely, if a horse could be removed and no gap appeared, that horse should not be included.

Without horses, my necklace is simply a string. I've had the necklace made and each fetish is hand-carved in turquoise stone. This means that each one is unique, just as the horses in my life were unique. The stones represent those horses that contributed so much to who I am today. I invite the reader to get to know the horses in my life and share with me the joy that I found with them.

With Quebrade, winner of the German Oaks

GINGER

I n the life of every horseman, there can be just one first horse. In my case, his name was Ginger. He was around thirteen years old when I met him and I was two. I like to imagine our first meeting, myself an infant, not in any sense aware of what life had in store, while he was a true old professional. He was a retired ranch horse, a strawberry roan, born on the Uhl Ranch around 1924, and he had been shown in competition at ranch-hand gatherings in the late 1920s. God only knows what his breeding was. He appeared to be part Thoroughbred and of part Spanish descent, but he had a little feather on his leg to suggest that maybe there was a draught horse somewhere in his family tree. He was about 15.2 hands in height and weighed around 1,150 pounds – he was no pony.

I don't have any memories of the start of our relationship, I was too young, but my mother told me that I rode Ginger by myself during my third year and I do have clear recollections of people exclaiming, 'That boy is only three, and look at him ride!' Apparently, I was able to walk, trot and canter. I had every advantage – my parents lived and worked on the Salinas Rodeo Competition Grounds, which comprised over two thousand acres of land just outside the city of Salinas. This wasn't exactly a rural landscape, though – it was covered with buildings, but all of them to do with horses. There was a full-sized show ring with raised seating, there were hundreds of box stalls, there was every

I won my first trophy on 25 June 1939, riding Ginger in the Junior Stock Horse Class. The prize was presented to me by actress Jane Withers

size of corral and enclosure, and a set of breeding barns. This land had been gifted to the city of Salinas and the condition of the bequest was that it was to be used as a riding facility by the townspeople. My family lived and worked at this establishment, training horses and running a riding school, so horses were part of our lives, twenty-four hours a day. It was in many ways perfect for a young child who liked horses, but it was also a lot of work and my father was a hard taskmaster. People had to be tough in those days. We were bang in the middle of the Great Depression and the Second World War was looming.

On 15 June 1939, when I was four, my father entered Ginger and me in a junior stock-horse competition in San Juan Bautista, a small community some twenty-five miles from where we lived in Salinas. When it came to my turn the judges asked me to complete an elementary reining course. Ginger did a couple of figure of eights complete with flying lead changes, cantered down to the end of the arena, stopped on his mark, settled and made the half turn left. He cantered to the other end, stopped, settled and made the half turn right. Then he cantered to the centre, stopped and backed up eight to ten steps. When we left the arena I had a great big smile on my face, thinking I had done it all on my own. The truth was, of course, that Ginger had done it. We still have grainy film footage of Ginger executing those manoeuvres and when I watch it now, I can see how I was just a passenger. Ginger did it all on his own.

We won the trophy, which was half as tall as me. Jane Withers, a child movie star of the time, presented it. She was always a light-hearted girl in her films, bringing laughter to everyone. Later, she became famous nationally as 'Josephine the Plumber' in a long-running TV advertising campaign. Even today I can relive the intense excitement I felt back then as I accepted the trophy from her, and I still have it on a shelf at home. The brass work is a little tarnished and the joints are loose, so it doesn't stand quite straight any more – a lot like me – but I treasure it, as you may imagine. The inscription reads: 'Champion, Children's Division, M. Roberts, aged 4.' Ginger's name isn't mentioned.

Ginger was more than my teacher; he also fulfilled the role of adoptive parent. Human infants are vulnerable. They need protection from the dangers of life and parents are meant to be their protectors. They have a responsibility to feed and care for a child not yet capable of providing for itself. While my mother was both nurturing and protective, my father wasn't. He was cruel to me and I was afraid of him. I was to discover later, through my Aunt Alice, his sister, that a much worse brutality was the order of the day in his own childhood.

I learned well before my third birthday how to escape from that cruelty – by running to Ginger. While riding Ginger, it seemed that my father couldn't catch me. Ginger's flying hooves took me away from the world of whips and beatings and the aggressive words that hurt more than any beating could, and in his stall I could hide with a friend who protected me and seemed to care for me.

With my mother's help, I even slept in his stall from time to time, when her body language somehow communicated to me that it would be better if I weren't in the house. My bed was in Ginger's hay manger and I was kept warm by an old-fashioned canvas sleeping bag. I suppose, although I don't know, that she told my father I was somewhere else. I don't think he knew.

The Second World War changed everyone's lives. Ginger and I were no exception. A stranger turned up at the gates, wearing a business suit and carrying a briefcase – a rare event in itself. My brother Larry and I watched this man as he talked with my mother and father. They showed him around. He examined the box stalls, and paid particular attention to the perimeter fencing. He completed measurements and made notes in a little book. At the ages of six and seven, Larry and I were old enough to know that something was going on.

It turned out that he was a representative of the United States government. A month later, a letter arrived informing us that the United States military was requisitioning the Salinas Rodeo Competition Grounds in order to convert it into an internment camp for Japanese-American citizens. We would have to move out immediately and, worse, my parents would be forced to get rid of forty to fifty horses.

This was bewildering. A whole section of the community was to be imprisoned here, the stables converted into basic living accommodation. Soldiers with guns would be manning the gates. Some of the Japanese children were our classmates and suddenly they were imprisoned. There was rationing of food, and some of my uncles were now in uniform and being sent to the far corners of the world.

Worse was to come. We had to shrink our operation dramatically and move into a rented house within the city of Salinas. There was no time, money or resources to maintain all the horses. Petrol was rationed. No one could afford transport. Horsemeat was required to boost the war effort. Everyone was in a hurry.

A stream of vehicles turned up to collect our horses and ship them to a killing plant in Crow's Landing, California. Ginger was among them. When they got there, they were unloaded and moved up a ramp with the aid of an electric prod. A steel door lifted and closed behind each one. Behind that door, Ginger was killed.

I had been with Ginger for many hours, every day of my life, between 1937 and 1942. He was the cave I had hidden in for safety, he was the tree I had climbed to play, he was the blanket I had rolled myself up in for comfort, and he was my partner in winning my first trophy. Suddenly he was gone, and his fate was unthinkable. I felt betrayed by every human being in my life – by the American government, by the Japanese and especially by my parents. I cried uncontrollably, night after night. I tried to understand the complications of war, but no matter how hard I worked at it, I could never justify the death of this eighteen-year-old strawberry roan that had so much life left in him.

The loss of Ginger made me realize how valuable friendships are. He is naturally the first stone in my necklace. I don't remember the first time I rode him – he simply rises into my life. I loved Ginger as much as any child has ever loved his first horse.

BROWNIE

We moved out of our home on the Salinas Rodeo Competition Grounds and into the town itself. My father had a new job, as a policeman. We rented an old house at the corner of Church and San Luis, 347 Church Street. It was a three-bedroomed, framed structure, costing $35 a month. In addition, my father rented a farmer's barn about two miles away on Villa Street, on the edge of town. It was there that we kept the few horses we could have while awaiting our return to the real world of horsemanship. We had a stallion named Johnny Stewart, a mare called Babe and an offspring of hers sired by Johnny Stewart. There were a few others around owned by clients of my father.

We were at war – I remember my mother bringing a world globe into my room and showing me the size of Japan and the size of the United States. She told me that this mess would be cleared up in a few months and we would be back on the Competition Grounds, living once more with our horses. She didn't show me Germany or Italy, and I really didn't know the extent of the world war until we had been in it for a year or so. I had four uncles in uniform, and I knew that one of them was in the South Pacific. The second was in the Navy, the third was a pilot somewhere near India and the fourth was in the infantry and fighting in Belgium. We wouldn't return to the Competition Grounds in a few months. The war kept us from our home until 1947.

In our old house I had grown used to hiding from my father, and under our new circumstances that hadn't changed. He worked shifts, choosing mostly to work at nights – the graveyard shift – and I was always busy checking my pocket-watch, keeping tabs on where he was, when he'd be back, when he'd be gone. It hung from my belt on a leather thong and it was in and out of my jeans twenty times a day. I still have that pocket-watch. My grandfather gave it to me. It's silver, marked 'Waltham', with Roman numerals, and railroad issue, so it's pretty much unbreakable. I give these details because it was the most important instrument to me at this time, telling me when my father would appear, and when he'd have to leave. To this day, I'm told I've got an obsessive relationship with time. I always know what time it is, give or take a minute or so.

With hindsight, I can see that my parents recognized the traumatic effect on me of Ginger's death, and wanted to help me recover. My father began to introduce into his conversation a young, brown mustang that he called Brownie, and my mother kept hinting that I needed a younger horse – why not Brownie?

Of course, I disliked Brownie. No one could – or should – replace Ginger.

After a while, though, I realized I couldn't blame Brownie for something he knew nothing about. Only human beings could be blamed for what had happened. I began to take an interest in him.

Brownie was very much the classic cross between the Thoroughbred and the mustang. He stood about 15.1 hands and weighed approximately 1,050 pounds. Most of the pure mustangs were less than 14.2 hands and a large one might reach 1,100 pounds. Brownie had the head and neck of a typical Thoroughbred but shorter coupled with thicker conformation. He had the look of a quality horse with a finer coat and a more elegant neck and head presentation than any pure mustang that I have seen. He was a dark mahogany brown all over with a jet-black mane and tail and black points. He had a few white hairs between his eyes but you had to look hard to find them. He was probably bred as the result of the remount project, which was an initiative conducted by the United States government to produce cavalry horses. It entailed releasing domestic stallions with mustang mares in order to achieve offspring that were larger than most mustangs and capable of being cavalry mounts. They even put some draught horses out there to produce the size and strength necessary to pull the large cannons. Brownie's father was probably a Thoroughbred.

I started to become attached to Brownie and so, of course, now there arose an additional responsibility on my part – I had to hide Brownie from my father. In my view, he was just as cruel to Brownie as he was to me and I had to keep Brownie away from him.

In fact, my father was only using the standard methods of the time, and it's worth going into their background, particularly since these methods are still being used in many parts of the world.

When the Spaniards first came to what we now know as the United States, there were literally millions and millions of buffalo, antelope and deer, but no horses – not one. The Spanish brought horses with them. Slowly, over time, some of these horses broke free, were let go or stolen by the Indians. Despite a vast array of predators – mountain lion, wolves and bears were all able to bring down adult horses – some of them survived and began to breed. We've come to know them as the mustang, a word that comes from 'mestengo', meaning wild thing in Spanish.

The only way the people knew of dealing with horses was the Spanish way, and the Spanish cowboys, or 'vaqueros' as they were called, used incredibly harsh methods. It's no accident that the term 'break' came to be accepted as a name for the process of subduing them. They broke the horses' will to fight, and they demanded obedience or they would cause great pain. One of the techniques involved the tying up of the horse's legs. The most common method was to truss one hind leg at a time to the neck and shoulders. The hind leg was held about a foot off the ground, which required the horse to stand on three legs. The idea was that the horse should fight against the rope until his will was broken – and then he'd stop fighting.

Sure enough, I watched my father employ similar methods with Brownie and the other horses in his care – it was nothing unusual. If Brownie shied at a piece of bag blowing across the path, my father would 'sack him out', as it was known. Brownie hated this punishment more than any other. My father would place a large rope around his neck and then drop it through a heavy halter. Next he'd tie Brownie to a sturdy post, restraining him with unbreakable equipment. He'd use another heavy rope to force one hind leg off the ground so it became virtually impossible for Brownie to move without falling. He'd attach a large piece of canvas or similar scary object to a rope about thirty feet long and, standing twenty feet or so from Brownie, he would throw the frightening object at him. Brownie would panic and try to flee, resulting in his falling and often injuring himself. The pain that Brownie suffered through this procedure seemed to make him even more determined to fight back, harder and harder. But he could never win.

It was during one of these sessions that my father decided to use a crinkly type of crepe paper used to wrap lettuce in boxes. It made, for Brownie, an awful sound that drove him out of his mind. He was frightened of the sound of paper until the day he died.

As a rule, my father slept from nine or ten in the morning until around three or four in the afternoon. With the help of my pocket-watch, I could judge when he would be around and so when to take Brownie to a back area and bit him up – a technique for leaving him to wander free with his tack on – so I could keep him from my father's sight. Otherwise, I'd ride him down the dirt tracks or in the fields on the edge of town, working with him and waiting for a time when he and I could go back safely.

I was escaping, and I was making sure, as much as possible, that Brownie escaped with me. We were in flight from pain and aggression and that flight took us to some places that otherwise we would probably never have gone. It accelerated my growing up, and it drove me to become a more effective horseman. I became responsible for some important duties beginning around the age of eight. I walked to the Villa Street barn and fed the horses before going to school. The Sacred Heart grammar school was only about a mile from there. I left work clothes at the barn, as our school required a uniform. I could walk back after school, change and ride Brownie for hours on end.

As soon as I was able to ride without my parents being worried that I

Brownie and me on a practice day at Villa Street Stable, 1945

might be injured, I was mostly left alone with Brownie. My father had a full schedule and when he decided it wasn't necessary for him to school Brownie any longer, without a word being spoken Brownie became my horse. We worked hard and we practised hard, Brownie and me. We weren't just running away now, we were running towards something as well – we were aiming for success in competition, once the war was over. Horse shows and rodeos had been suspended, but we could see the time coming when they would be revived.

This was a way of preventing trouble with my father. Audiences meant safety because violence towards me was hidden from public view. Horse competitions would provide a safe haven for Brownie and me and the more successful we were in front of an audience, the safer we'd be. If Brownie and I could achieve good results in a show, it would reflect well on my parents' business, which would have to be started up again in earnest once the war was over. I made sure to keep on telling my father about Brownie's and my progress in roping and in executing the manoeuvres necessary for Western events. If he hadn't heard about it, he'd have been on my case. He would have probably taken over Brownie's training programme. At the same time, he greeted any success we had with criticism instead of approval, and I dare say this created an even stronger desire in me to win.

By the time we returned to the Competition Grounds in 1947, Brownie and I were a team. We'd had over four years to prepare and, believe you me, we were ready to compete. I was twelve and there simply was no other twelve-year-old in the United States able to take on Brownie and me. We won one championship after another. In addition to our preparation, Brownie was talented and along with his ability came a forgiving attitude that I didn't even appreciate until much later in life. Brownie was able to forgive the brutal treatment of his past and remain generous.

I learned to rope on Brownie. While he was a better horse for heeling than heading, he was good either way. Heeling means that after a partner ropes the head of the running steer, Brownie and I would attempt to catch both hind legs. This was, and still is, the method used on the ranches of the western United States to doctor cattle. If you find a sick or lame animal miles from any corral or holding facility, the best way to doctor him is to head and heel. The horses maintain the tension on the ropes to hold him while someone performs the necessary medical procedure. Brownie and I helped with the doctoring of a lot of cattle, mostly to administer medication for pink eye. If you don't medicate early and regularly, the animal can lose the sight of the affected eye. Often in the spring we had to doctor for bloat, a problem that occurs when feed is plentiful. Cattle will blow up with gas and will die if you don't relieve them of the excess.

Brownie and I won many team ropings together and I suppose I practised that event more than any other throughout the late forties. We had a little game we played. I would put a steer in a square corral and Brownie and I would stand in the middle of the corral while the steer inevitably found his way to a corner. We would allow the steer to turn, with his head towards us, and then we would run towards it at top speed. When the steer moved, Brownie would do an immediate U turn, putting me in a position to rope the hind legs. This meant that no header was necessary, and the animal didn't have to be pulled for practice.

Brownie became very proficient at this game and taught me much about handling cattle from horseback and how to encourage horses to perform because they want to. I was able to rope for half an hour or more each day while never pulling the steer's legs or causing it any discomfort. Brownie would dance in place in a piaffe-like movement and then, with a subtle cue from me, he'd make his run. Brownie seemed to love this game and we played it a lot.

In addition, there were the ever-present gymkhana events. Musical chairs, pole bending and races of every description were a vital part of the junior horse shows of the forties and the fifties; they were important in the total scheme of things. Each of the junior competitions offered a championship, which they called the All-Around. This went to the winner of the most accumulated points. The gymkhana events contributed the same number of points as the stock-horse class or Western equitation.

The All-Around at any given horse show would provide the winner with the largest and most important trophy of the day, but, more importantly, the points awarded went towards county, state and national championships. I was determined to win the All-Around at every gymkhana I entered. Brownie was absolutely incredible to ride in the musical chairs. You might think this is just a game of chance and if you're near an empty chair when the music stops, you're in luck. This is not the case. Brownie knew how to stack the horses up behind him, cantering extremely slowly if he needed to, or running all out to stay in front of the competitors. No matter when the music stopped, Brownie left me with chairs available and I recall winning something of the order of twenty-two straight musical-chairs events.

Brownie carried me a long, long way. Between 1947 and 1952, from twelve to seventeen years old, he and I travelled approximately 250,000 miles in trailers, trucks and even an old railroad car. Brownie accompanied me from the top to the bottom of California, and ventured with me into Arizona, New Mexico, Nevada and even south-eastern Oregon on one trip. Sure, there were other horses in my life during these years. I entered competitions for jumping and for gaits as well as those in the Western division. I rode dozens of other horses, including Mischief, Burgundy and an assortment of American Saddlebreds, but at this formative stage of my life, Brownie was my horse and he knew it.

We had great adventures out of the arena and chased wild cattle at night, in total darkness, on the Laguna Seca Ranch near Salinas. A lady called Dorothy Tavernetti paid us by the head. Brownie was an incredible partner in this task. We spent weeks following mustangs, and he would assist me when we got home, working with the wild horses in the home corrals.

I had been competing on Brownie for four years or so when I noticed that his performances were tailing off a bit. No matter how hard I tried, we just seemed to be drifting downwards in our scores. As it turned out, trying so hard was the cause of our problems. I wanted perfection every day of the week and I wasn't able to see or hear Brownie's side of the issue.

Professional trainers advised me that Brownie was jaded. He was becoming sour because of the gruelling practice schedule that a young, over-enthusiastic rider was putting him through. He needed a rest.

I took the advice that I was given, and I had a conversation with Brownie. Of course, the conversation was with myself really but he was there and I talked to him as though he understood every word. 'I'm going to ease up on our practice schedule, and if you'll promise to give me a hundred per cent on Saturday and Sunday, I'll allow those Tuesday, Wednesday and Thursday workouts to be much easier.' Brownie didn't understand English but he certainly responded to the good advice given to me by those trainers. His performances immediately improved, and shortly after this decision we marked the high point of our career.

I recall going back to Brownie's stall and thanking him (in English) for teaching me a good lesson. I made a pledge that I would listen to the signals he gave me, that I would try my hardest to know what he was thinking, to talk his language, if you will. Now, I realize the importance of that place and time. Brownie was a teacher, a counsellor and a motivator.

Brownie and I were approximately the same age – seventeen years old – when we rode down one day to play our game in the square corral with the steer. We went through the regular procedures of preparing for our session and I noticed nothing out of the ordinary as we began to practise. After seven or eight forays into the corner, we were standing in the centre of the corral preparing for our next run. Brownie was excited, as usual, and when the steer was right, he took me to the appropriate spot just as he always did. On this particular occasion, however, as he made his turn to set me up for my throw, I felt an unusual movement. Brownie nearly came to a full halt, and then I felt him spread his legs and stagger. I recall looking down and wondering what was going on. Brownie leapt forward and crashed to the ground. I was thrown clear.

I got up, in a state of shock, and stood looking at Brownie. He was motionless. I don't know how I got there but I remember putting the back of my hand to his fore flank just under the cinch, trying to feel a heartbeat. I cupped my hands over his nose and begged him to breathe for me. I placed my palms on his side and pushed for many long minutes, hoping for a miracle.

It was no good. Brownie was dead. I stood up and watched as his eyes took on a silvery, opaque look. I felt the silence and emptiness of life without him.

No rendering plant was going to take Brownie. I was going to bury him where he died, right there on the Competition Grounds. I got hand tools and began to dig a grave. I worked for several hours – the ground was as hard as concrete.

I vividly recall that my father came when he got the news. I suppose he understood the loss of a horse more than he understood any other of life's challenges. He put his hand on my shoulder and told me how sorry he was. He said he knew how much Brownie had meant to me. It was the only time he ever treated me with compassion. I had lost a friend but I experienced the one single moment of kindness I had ever received from my father.

After ten minutes or so, he went to the house and made a telephone call to a man by the name of Kennedy who had a construction company. He made arrangements for a mechanical digger to be brought to the site, so a proper grave could be dug for Brownie, a horse too wonderful for words.

In 1999, some forty-seven years after Brownie's death, I happened to be in Salinas when I was told they were tearing down the stalls on the old Competition Grounds. I went up there to have a last look and found that both Ginger's and Brownie's stalls were still standing – the mechanical grabs hadn't quite reached that far. I approached the foreman and told him I had been raised there, and asked would he mind if I took a board or two from a couple of the stalls, as mementoes. 'Hell,' he said, 'I wish you'd turned up earlier. We've got to pay to haul this stuff away. Take what you want.' I pulled off a board from Brownie's and one from Ginger's. I have them to this day, tucked out of sight so no one mistakes them for firewood.

Brownie's journey through life stopped that afternoon, but he started me off in the direction I've followed ever since. Brownie and I ran from aggression and violence. We ran as far and as hard as possible in order to escape and, in my work with horses, I've kept going the same way – away from aggression, pain and violence.

Even as I write this, I'm working with a horse that is phobically frightened of plastic shopping bags – just like Brownie was scared of that crinkled paper. With the approach I've used on this horse, after just two short sessions I can rub him all over with plastic bags. I constantly rub his head and congratulate him as he allows this awful object into his life. Not one moment of pain was used in treating this troubled horse.

Brownie encouraged me to see the world through his eyes, to respect his needs and to realize that even our best friends will be less than perfect at times. Brownie needed me to protect him from the traditional world of harsh horsemanship. He was certainly one of the main reasons I've dedicated my life to non-violent training. He was the perfect horse to become that stone in my necklace following Ginger. He was responsible for showing me that life is a two-way street, receiving my protection and rewarding me with outstanding performances week after week. Brownie caused the horse world to think that I was a champion when all the time he was the champion, tugging the best out of me. The memory of Brownie will never wane so long as I live.

Today, as I sit signing autographs for people who come to my demonstration events, I often recognize that certain look in the eyes of a child who has a wonderful horse at home. I know that look because I was just the same. When I had Ginger and then Brownie, I had a wonderful horse at home, too.

MISCHIEF
AND DAN TACK

I first saw Mischief on the day she was born in the Villa Street barn – a dark
brown filly, struggling to control her legs and take her first steps. The barn
was my environment, my place. I'd been mucking out, feeding and grooming
there since the age of eight. Now the magic spell cast by the new foal aroused
protective instincts in me. I felt almost as much responsibility for her as her
own mother did.

I watched Mischief grow. She was strong and confident, enjoying the
protection and nurturing that is the birthright of every infant. Yet with each
inch she grew I felt more dread because when she reached her full height, just
over 14 hands, she would be ready for breaking in. If the normal course of
events was allowed to happen, her legs would be tied and she'd be sacked
out until the fight was taken out of her. She would feel the full force of the
world of human misunderstanding. I was determined to save her from that
experience if I possibly could.

With Brownie, I had managed to get him out of my father's clutches some
time after he'd been subjected to the traditional methods of horse breaking.
Maybe I could save Mischief from violence and pain right from the outset.

My father was still working in the police force and he was preoccupied
with that and with the newly restarted riding school back on the Competition
Grounds. I manoeuvred it so that I got his permission to start and train
Mischief all on my own. He expected me to tie her legs and do the sacking out
– he'd shown me how many times. I was aged fourteen.

My father had a predictable pattern. He'd be home from the night shift around seven in the morning and I would make sure I was working hard cleaning stalls because he would go into a kind of frenzy for an hour or two, to get the day up and running. He'd go to bed around nine and sleep until three or four. That was my window for starting to train Mischief by myself.

I didn't use ropes, posts or whips. Instead, I very patiently asked for Mischief's cooperation and trust. She was accustomed to human handling and it wasn't long before I was leaning my weight over her back, getting her used to it. I familiarized her with the saddle and bridle, allowing her all the time she wanted. It wasn't such a big step for her when I suggested the saddle might rest on her back. She was wearing a halter and hadn't endured a moment's pain.

Winning a hackamore competition on Mischief, 1949

All this time I worked at keeping her away from the house, and trained with as much privacy as possible. None of the brutality that I had observed in the traditional methods was necessary, not for one minute, not for any reason. My father's schedule worked to my advantage, and I believe that by the time he saw Mischief, she was doing well enough for him not to question my tactics. I remember him making such comments as, 'She's just a natural.'

Mischief progressed through the first year of training exceptionally well. Short and stocky as she was, it was not easy for her to express fluid athleticism. I was pleased that she could accomplish flying changes better than Brownie – it gave me confidence that Brownie's difficulties with them were not entirely due to my inept training.

When I first began to ride her, we had been back at the Competition Grounds for about a year. In July of 1949, I entered Mischief in open competition – that's to say against all comers, adults included – in the hackamore class. Introduced by the Spanish, the hackamore is a bitless rawhide noseband requiring a high degree of responsiveness from the horse to execute the manoeuvres necessary for competition. We rode proudly into the ring and went through our paces, executing flying lead changes and doing our stops and turns. I felt the audience's eyes burning into me.

We won. I remember so well her picture on the cover of the local newspaper – a good advertisement for our riding school, so it kept us both safe from my father. By now, I knew better than to expect any praise or encouragement from him. At fourteen, it was a strange, contradictory feeling to win in open competition, against adults, but to receive just a few surly criticisms from my father – a mixture of triumph and disappointment.

Mischief was the first competition horse that I trained from the outset and she proved that it wasn't necessary to be brutal to achieve top-class performances. I showed her a dozen or so times only, but she was part of my team in 1949.

Shortly after her picture appeared in the local paper, my father came to me with a proposal to sell Mischief. He'd had an offer of $2,000 from a lady by the name of Ruth Wilson. Mrs Wilson would leave Mischief with us in training, which made it all the sweeter. He went on to say that I needed a better horse than Brownie or Mischief if I was going to go for the National Championship in Horsemastership.

Dan Tack carried me to the National Championship in Horsemastership, 1950

A Texan was boarding horses with us for a short time, including a beautiful dun gelding called Dan Tack, by Arizona Dan out of a Hard Tack mare. These names are among the earliest registered Quarter Horses. If we sold Mischief, my father offered to buy Dan Tack. My mother and he were willing to put up the additional $500 needed. I thought Dan Tack was a beautiful horse with a lot of potential. Everyone was waiting for my agreement and I felt involved in the deal. Money was changing hands, judgements were being passed, proposals made. I nodded my head. OK, I agreed to the sale. I was dealing in horses.

Dan Tack generously carried me to my first National Championship, and it was through his efforts that I realized I had sufficient talent to compete at world-class level. His encouragement sent me forward in a way that might never have happened in his absence.

Mischief stayed with us for many more years and was the riding horse for Ruth Wilson, who loved and treated her well. Mischief was important in my life for two distinct reasons. The first is that she showed me that harsh treatment is simply not necessary to create a willing partner in a horse. The other is that she represented my first small step towards becoming a professional. She opened the door the first inch. Horses were not only to be my life and my passion; they were going to be my livelihood, too.

NO-NAME MUSTANG

I never knew the name of this horse. He didn't have one when I met him because he'd just been rounded up and brought down from the ranges of Nevada, and I have no idea where he wound up after the few days that I'm going to describe. None the less, he affected my entire life.

To try to explain what went on, I have to go back one year. In 1948, due to circumstances surrounding our return to the Competition Grounds, I was asked to go along with several adults to northern Nevada to assist in the yearly round-up of mustangs, which would be used in the wild-horse race during the Salinas Rodeo. During this trip I developed a real enthusiasm for discovering how these vulnerable flight animals communicated with one another in the wild. Having read everything I could lay my hands on regarding the development of the horse, I was bubbling over with curiosity about how they survived in a harsh environment.

High up on the Nevada ranges, I found I could gain enough trust for family groups to allow me close enough to read their responses to one another through binoculars. I observed that they had a communication system, a silent one, made up of gestures rather than sounds. Silence was important if they were not to attract predators. The ear, the neck, the tongue, the shoulders and the tail of the horse were most often used to communicate with one another.

In particular, I noted the gestures used by the dominant mare to discipline the youngsters. They were 100 per cent predictable and measurable – punishment for any misdemeanour was to be driven away, so the offender would have to stand outside the herd, in grave danger from predators. Only when the dominant mare received the correct signals of apology – the adolescent's ear locked on to her, licking and chewing and a dropping of its head low to the ground – would she allow it back in to the safety of the group.

I also began to realize how important it was for them to understand the gestures of predators. They read the feet of the cat and the shoulders of the bear just as efficiently as they read the gestures of the horses in their own family.

Fast forward to the following year, 1949, and my second trip to the Nevada ranges. Having confirmed my observations from the previous year, I was anxious to get home to see the mustangs we had captured close up. At the back of my mind I had some idea about trying out these signals for myself. Would a mustang respond to me in the same way as I had seen them respond to their own kind? Could we exchange thoughts and signals? If so, we would have inter-species communication.

As I remember it, four of us returned home a day ahead of the mustangs. Around a hundred and fifty of them arrived late the next afternoon and we spent the better part of two hours sorting them into pens. I believe we gave them about three days to eat, drink and rest.

Feeling like I was the luckiest fourteen-year-old boy in history, I rode Brownie down to the corrals. I wanted to choose a subject and test my theories. These large corrals were divided into two columns of enclosures, separated by an alleyway about 12 feet wide and including a double-sized corral at both ends (see page 31). The fences were at least eight feet high and the whole complex was painted dark green, so they were referred to as the green corrals. I rode Brownie into the entrance/exit lane, tied his reins back to the saddle and began to walk between the corrals, looking at the mustangs left and right and watching out for injuries or illness.

I stopped at the gate of corral number two. The cowboys had allocated about ten stallions to this enclosure and, as I stood there, my instincts tugged at me to go in and get closer to this small group of young, healthy mustangs. I don't think any horseman can walk through a group such as this without sorting them in his mind, scanning the herd for that outstanding individual. A dark bay mustang caught my eye immediately. I was drawn to him as if we were magnetized. He didn't seem to be nearly as interested in me as I was in him; he was merely tolerant of my presence. This was my no-name mustang.

Acting as I had seen the mustangs do, I zigzagged through the group eight or ten times, allowing my eyes to drift away from the dark bay stallion when he gave me his attention, and conversely piercing his eyes with mine when he moved away. I was barely aware of the other horses in the pen.

So far, so good. I had the horse to work with but I wanted him on his own. I fetched Brownie and we filtered the other horses out.

The next two hours must rank among the most important times I've spent with any horse in my entire life. I walked into the corral and waited for him to settle following the excitement of seeing his friends separated off. As I walked towards him, he began trotting or cantering around the outskirts of the enclosure. Along one side, he had the comfort of some other mustangs that he could see through the fence. Along this stretch, he focused on them. As he moved further around, he was obliged to lose sight of them and instead he began to concentrate on me. His ear locked on me. I knew that sign from my observations of his kin in the wild. It meant that he was according me the same respect as he would any predator, or the matriarch of his family group.

The next time he went around, he found his friends over the fence again, and as he left them behind his ear locked on me once more. Then he began a vigorous licking and chewing action with his mouth and my heart practically stopped beating. This was an attempt to negotiate with me. I was sure it must be. It was the same signal that I had seen on many occasions in the wild. If so, it meant this mustang was asking for my help in rescuing him from an uncomfortable situation – he was talking to me and I could understand.

Then, as he went around the fourth or fifth time, moving at a full trot, his head dropped until his nose was bouncing only inches from the ground. Any lingering doubts disappeared. There was no mistake. This was the exact combination of signals I had observed in the wild, in the same order and to an even greater degree. I was elated. At the same time I felt a flash of anger. I asked myself who was going to apologize to all the horses that had gone before for such utter and complete misunderstanding. It was clear now that horses enjoyed being our partners. They were willing to cooperate with us, if we would just communicate and request rather than demand.

After a few minutes, I wondered what would happen if I turned away from him and acted as I had seen the matriarch do when she received those same signals – give up eye contact and turn away.

The mustang stopped. I glanced over my shoulder. He was looking at me face on. I turned away and waited. A moment later, I became aware that he was walking towards me. No more than a yard away, he stopped. I was holding my breath. Would this wild horse attack me? No. I reached out to try to touch him but he moved off sharply. When I turned my back on him again, he came and stood at my shoulder. I took a pace or two and he followed. I kept going. This mustang was following me, step for step. I stopped, he stopped. I was exhilarated. I was communicating with a wild mustang. In showing him that I understood his language, I had gained his trust.

I wanted to tell my father what I had done but I knew him to be prone to violence whenever I failed to follow his instructions to the letter. My mother was ever vigilant and quick to warn me when she sensed danger. In this case, I received that warning and realized that I could be heading for trouble, so I kept quiet. I tried to tell my brother and various trainers who were working their horses at the Competition Grounds at the time but no one wanted to know. I couldn't believe it. Not one person took me seriously. It was a fake, a fraud and it was dangerous, they said. I shouldn't be messing around like that or I would certainly end up dead, trampled under the hooves of a mustang. I decided I had to keep this thing to myself until I thought someone would believe me. I didn't realize it would take forty years.

There's a strong case for this mustang being not just the most important horse in my life, but one of the most important horses that ever lived. His message would help the world to understand the language and needs of these wonderful partners who share the earth with us.

A diagram of the corrals where I worked with No-name and many other mustangs

BUSTER

The high desert ranges of Nevada create a unique landscape. The hills are stunningly beautiful, with variations in the thin soil making layered patterns. As far as the eye can see, deep barrancas, or small canyons, sprout stunted and tortured trees, and small scrub plants, primarily sage, are everywhere. The night sky seems to go on forever, and the stars are so vivid I used to think I could reach out from my sleeping bag and pluck them with my fingertips. The thin air means the nights are freezing but, at sun up, the cold changes to warmth as if someone has flicked a switch. In summertime the heat can easily reach scorching levels.

In the summer of 1952 I was seventeen years old. Once again, I had the opportunity to take part in the mustang round-up and, as usual, the Campbell Ranch supplied some Indian hands to help us. It was a yearly routine and everyone was well practised and knew what to do.

On this particular occasion, I had some spare days when I wouldn't have to be working, and I had a plan. Over the last three years, since my encounter with the no-name mustang, I had been developing and practising my ideas about communicating with horses. I called my system join-up, and I wanted to see if I could persuade a horse to accept his first saddle, bridle and rider while still in the wild. I wouldn't use a corral or pen of any kind. I would form a partnership with a wild horse on his home ground, using the technique that I knew by now wasn't a fluke, or a fake. On the contrary, it worked every time. Then I would ride this wild mustang home. I was convinced that I could do it.

I went scouting among the wild herds and eventually found a strong bay colt, probably four or five years old, showing a lot of Andalusian characteristics – high action in front, feathers on his fetlocks and a muscular neck and shoulder. He had large, black eyes with an excited glint to them. Horsemen might say he had an intelligent eye. His entire appearance appealed to me. He was the one.

As I cut him away from the herd, he was a magnificent sight. His neck was arched, his nose held high and he stuck his tail straight up so that the hair flowed down over his hips. He ran as fast as he could and I followed, convinced I could negotiate with this young horse and persuade him to trust me and want to be near me. This would be the ultimate test of join-up.

He had a short, powerful stride, totally unlike that of the Thoroughbred. Working to bend him in different directions, I was essentially driving him away, and we settled into a pattern. I knew what to look for, the ear, the licking and chewing and the head dipping to a level near the ground. My experience at home with his brothers and sisters had taught me so much about interpreting the language of equus, as I had come to call it.

At home I used a circular corral around 50 feet (16 metres) in diameter with solid-wall fencing. The horse's flight was not interrupted because there were no corners, and no distractions could claim the horse's attention from outside. The round pen concentrated the process whereas in the wilderness there were hundreds of miles of territory in every direction, with no fences of any kind, and so there was no immediate need for Buster to negotiate with me. I needed patience. This wasn't going to be measured in minutes, as it was at home. I kept on pushing him away, driving him out on his own.

On the second day, it happened. He displayed those signals that told me he was asking to come in and talk to me about this. After some very patient negotiations, I could drop a rope around this proud mustang's neck and lead him around. He was still wild, but seemed to be trying hard for me. Within another hour or so, I was dropping a long rope over his rear quarters and he kicked with a purpose. When he kicked, I found myself saying, 'Hey, Buster. What are you trying to do?' That's why I called him Buster. Soon the kicking subsided and I was able to advance to the next step.

I continued to progress – but very slowly, very calmly – through the procedures that I had developed with the mustangs back in Salinas. The girth strap, the long lines and then the saddle were accepted a little at a time, with plenty of breaks in between for him to settle and get used to the idea of being in partnership with me. The first saddle I used on him was a Western saddle and it seemed to be unacceptable. He kicked at the stirrups and bucked but, after a while, his objections died down and he carried it with no great concern.

The following afternoon, I put one foot in the stirrup and gently lifted my weight on to it. I held the position and stroked his neck for a minute or so before easing my right foot to the ground again. I repeated the action a few times. Then I gave him a rest. After fifteen or twenty such repetitions, I leaned my hips well into the saddle and stayed up there. Buster moved a step at a time in a circular motion to the left, but he was calm and seemed ready to accept the idea of someone on his back. When the moment seemed right I slowly swung my right leg over his back and into the stirrup on the off side. I was riding him.

The area I chose to try riding Buster was sandy, with no dangerous stones. I had learned that if you are bucked off and injured out there by yourself, it can be life threatening. I had a twenty-five foot rope coiled in my belt and linked to Buster so that if he did buck me off I would have a chance of keeping hold of him. Horses have been lost in the wilderness wearing saddles and, although I was convinced I could make him want to stay with me, I was still just a green kid.

Buster wasn't gentle but, like so many mustangs, he didn't want to buck. He was touchy at first and would flinch and jump sideways with every movement of my hands or legs, but within twenty to thirty minutes he settled. The next day, I rode Buster straight out and down the trail. In that huge landscape I felt as if we were the centre of the universe. I rode Buster several different times that day, mounting and dismounting from either side.

On the morning of the fifth day, I began my trek back to the headquarters of the Campbell Ranch, where this adventure had begun. I rode my saddle horse most of the way to keep Buster fresh. Two miles from the ranch headquarters, and with no little sense of anticipation, I switched to Buster. I rode him at a trot, leading my saddle horse and my packhorse. I felt a sweet sense of accomplishment as Buster marched into that barnyard like he had been doing it all of his life.

A group of men were doctoring calves in a corral, some were working on a generator over by a barn, and others were coming out of the bunkhouse. They looked me over and asked what was going on. I told them what I had done and

I expected to see their expressions change, to hear questions. Instead, I was received with disbelief.

'You must have taken an already broken horse and salted the herd,' said one cowboy.

'Look at his feet,' I countered. 'He's never had a shoe on. You can see he's an out-and-out mustang.'

'I can see he's been out there, all right,' he said, 'but you were lucky enough to find one that someone else has gotten to first.'

This was the scepticism I had faced at home. 'Here we go again,' I thought, feeling angry and frustrated. I had achieved what I thought was a significant breakthrough in the way we dealt with horses and no one believed me. Maybe next year, I thought. When I was twenty-one, or when I had some kind of training establishment of my own, people would have to listen.

As I view it now, Mother Nature was working overtime. She'd sent me the no-name mustang and then she sent me a second mustang and asked me to convince the world they could be dealt with in a non-violent manner. Buster was unbelievably generous, and he worked hard to give me the evidence I needed to convince horsemen that violence was unnecessary. Something spiritual was hard at work to educate a young man to these principles. Buster, an American mustang, seemed willing to give up his freedom for a few days in an attempt to show me that I was on the right track. Once more I fell short at sending the message forward. Buster was only successful in validating these concepts to me, but to no one else. I released him back into the wild but Buster sent me forward with a life dedicated to leaving the world a better place for horses.

BERNIE

In 1955, when I was twenty, I was awarded a football scholarship to California Polytechnic University, which would cover my tuition and living expenses. However, a knee injury sustained at the end of my two-season football career at Hartnell College just prior to entering Cal Poly ended my participation in that sport and meant I couldn't fulfil the obligations of the scholarship. Instead, I trained and rode a few horses to supplement my income.

Although I enjoyed football, it wasn't the main reason I had chosen to go to Cal Poly. It might seem odd for someone outside the western United States, but I wanted to go there because the college had a rich history in inter-collegiate rodeo. Just as some other colleges pride themselves on their football, baseball or ice hockey, and Oxford and Cambridge Universities pride themselves on their rowing and rugby, Cal Poly has enjoyed a long history of excellence in rodeo. I was asked to join the travelling squad immediately. From October through to June I would be expected to travel to ten competitions in six states.

Rodeo evolved out of common working practices on ranches. Bulldogging, for instance, started out as a competition between cowboys to see who could get to a steer the quickest when it broke from a herd. These cowboys had to hold cattle bunched up together in the open landscape, sometimes for many hours, and a steer breaking out caused great excitement. There'd be rivalry over who could get to it first, jump from his horse and throw the steer to the ground barehanded. A black cowboy named Bill Picket developed the trick of leaping from his horse's back in full flight and wrapping his arms around the steer's horns. He would then bite the animal's upper lip. This was how British bulldogs brought down deer, so the event became known as bulldogging. Fortunately, the lip-biting part of it fell by the wayside.

Bulldogging, also known as steer wrestling, was to be my main event. It was like performing a judo throw on a 700-pound steer while running full out. Many cowboys are injured. The animals are much larger and stronger than any human and the man has just his God-given anatomy.

The steers used in bulldogging typically weigh between 600 and 800 pounds and must have a mature set of horns. They are often imported from Mexico where the sparse deserts produce animals with relatively small bodies and ample horn development. The primary cowboy has to ride past the left, or near side, of a running steer, stop him by leaping from the horse and grabbing his horns, and wrestle him to the ground with his bare hands. No ropes are involved. So that the steer doesn't duck away from the competitor, there is a second cowboy riding a horse on the right side of the steer, hoping to keep the animal in a straight line. The secondary cowboy is called the hazer and his horse is referred to as a haze horse.

Team roping is also a skill used every day on ranches. One cowboy would rope the steer's head, another would rope the heels and the animal would be laid out ready for any veterinary treatment that might be necessary. I had helped with doctoring many times on Brownie. In reality, the work is done at a gentle pace and with minimum stress – no one wants injuries to animals or cowboys. In the rodeo arena, however, where the gloves come off, it's a timed event.

My first competition for the Cal Poly rodeo team was in October in Eugene, Oregon. I needed a fast, responsive Quarter Horse, skilled enough in manoeuvring for me to rope the rear legs of a galloping steer. Brownie had been my educator in the art of roping. He was gone now, but right out of the blue came the answer to my prayers – Bernie.

Bernie was a little chestnut horse, originally from Arizona. He started out as my brother Larry's horse, but Larry joined the Navy and so Bernie was without a job to do, which was lucky for me. At 14.3 hands and weighing around 1,000 pounds, he was hard pressed to excel as a heading horse. Roping

OVERLEAF *A rare photo of me bulldogging on Bernie in Phoenix, Arizona*

the horns of a 600- or 700-pound steer and handling it so the heeler could throw his rope was generally reserved for those horses closer to 16.0 hands and weighing over 1,200 pounds.

However, Bernie fitted the bill for heeling, especially for an intercollegiate rodeo team. He was a natural heel horse and rapidly became extremely competent in that role. Even if the steer was swinging around on the end of the header's long rope, Bernie would chase that steer's tail and take every turn with my boot practically on the ground, he leaned in so far.

Also, because he'd originally been used as a heading horse, Bernie was a useful back up for other members of the team should that become necessary. He could assist in bulldogging if required as a good haze horse. In the language of professional rodeo, you'd call Bernie an all-around horse, which is exactly what team rodeo requires.

Bernie was an ideal travelling partner – tolerant and making the best of situations that weren't always comfortable. He was willing to accept and forgive my mistakes. I could leave him tied up to the side of the trailer while I made a few dollars, waiting at the bottom of icy roads to attach people's chains to their tyres. He probably saved my life, and certainly prevented a severe case of frostbite, when we were stranded together in an incredible snowstorm. His body warmth protected me while my travelling partner made a four-hour journey to buy a replacement tyre for one that had blown on our trailer. I may not have had any hands if Bernie's fore flanks hadn't kept them from freezing. As it was, I lost all the skin off my feet and ears in this near-death experience with nature.

Bernie stood by me, worked hard for me and was my good friend. He brought me luck. I was married to Bernie for four years, or that's what it felt like.

In fact, I was engaged to be married to Pat and the date was set for 16 June 1956. Then it turned out that Bernie and I might be expected to compete in the finals of the National Intercollegiate Rodeo Championships in Colorado on the same day. As the college year progressed, it began to look dangerous: Bernie and I accumulated a sufficient number of points to qualify for the finals and we had a chance of winning the world championship in team roping. Should I choose Bernie and the rodeo team or Pat and my future with her?

The team and the school were not entirely happy when I decided against making the trip to Colorado and to marry Pat instead but, on the other hand, they were happy for us.

During the previous six months of travelling, I had been setting up a little joke on my future in-laws. At every stop, I bought a postcard, wrote it out and addressed it and arranged for somebody to send it to my future mother-in-law after the wedding. I planned it so that a card would be arriving every five days or so during our honeymoon from a string of towns spread all over the western United States. On the cards, I mentioned the names of the classiest hotels I saw at each of the stops. I knew Pat's mother was concerned about her beautiful daughter marrying a cowboy with limited funds and I thought that this plan would give her great joy, and I was right. We later explained the joke and let her know that we had been staying in a little cabin on the beach at Carmel just twenty or so miles from Salinas.

I made the right choice. Pat and I have three grown-up children, Deborah, Laurel and Marty, and three grandchildren, Matthew, Adam and Loren. She has been more than a good wife to me, better than I could have imagined. We met when we were eight years old at the Sacred Heart grammar school, and we've been married now for forty-eight years.

Bernie made the trip to the championships, and assisted the team in acquiring a significant number of points. Greg Ward, a team-mate, rode Bernie into the arena to accept my saddle and trophy buckle. Greg told the announcer in front of the audience that Bernie was the horse with which I had earned the points and, since he was the only reason I had won anyway, they were honouring the correct individual.

Bernie was, indeed, a big part of my individual successes at Cal Poly but an even bigger part of the achievements of the team in general. He was just a little Arizona chestnut who will never be known as a major rodeo star. I don't know his sire or his dam but it doesn't matter. Bernie assisted many young people to become better competitors.

MISS TWIST

Miss Twist came into our lives around 1949 or '50. Blinding speed was the centrepiece of her existence. While control was in short supply with Miss Twist, her ability to transport a rider for a couple of hundred yards or so was incredible – it was like riding a rocket.

Initially, my father bought her to send her to the racetrack. In the western United States, they have regulation tracks for Quarter Horse racing and Miss Twist was pretty much the quickest vehicle on the face of the earth for the first 220 yards. Unfortunately, she ran out of steam at that point and slowed dramatically. Most Quarter Horse races ask for 350 yards.

Miss Twist came home from the racetrack at about the time I was going off to Cal Poly and my father asked me to take her with me and train her as a bulldogging horse. In bulldogging, the horse has to be fast for a maximum of 100 yards and most efforts require less than 50 yards of full speed. Miss Twist should be perfect.

When I began to train this rocket-like equine she quickly gained the attention of every potential bulldogger at Cal Poly but she was not a particularly good horse for a college rodeo team. She wasn't user friendly. Most of my team-mates were not specialists and Miss Twist was not the horse for inexperienced cowboys just trying their hand at bulldogging in pursuit of a few extra points.

Jack Roddy, who went on to become a world champion bulldogger and a member of the Cowboy Hall of Fame, rode her while on the team with me. I don't think he was ever very happy with riding what seemed like a runaway train past a slow-moving bovine and being expected to grab the horns as he went by. If you weren't ready for her seemingly uncontrollable speed, it was hard to concentrate on your bulldogging effort.

John W. Jones is said by many to be the greatest bulldogger who ever lived. Also a world champion and member of the Cowboy Hall of Fame, John has been the inspiration for many young bulldoggers, including his son, John Jr, who won the world championship three times. John Sr rode Miss Twist several times and I must say he made a gallant effort to get used to her but he still nicknamed her 'Misfit'. The name stuck with her for the rest of her career.

Once the rider said go, Miss Twist was on autopilot. There was no adjusting speed or using good judgement for a difficult surface or other environmental circumstances. She just went all out. She delivered me to many steers in the three and four second range, allowing me to win one bulldogging event after another.

The most memorable day in the life I lived with Miss Twist came when John W. and I decided to go to San Jose, California to practise for a day or so on Jack Roddy's ranch. Making the trip with us was Everett Muzio Jr, known by his friends as Junior Muzio. It was time to introduce him to Miss Twist.

John W. put Junior on her, made sure his stirrups were right and gave him a few words of advice.

'When you ask her to go, she goes,' warned John. 'Be ready and quick to jump the steer. Don't ride her by your steer without jumping because she will take you to the other end of the arena, and it will be a trip you'll never forget.'

Junior backed into the bulldogger's starting box, nodded his head and Miss Twist went from a standing start to full speed in about three strides. Junior went by the steer so fast that he hadn't even begun to prepare to jump. He sat up straight in the saddle and Miss Twist took him to the end of the arena, about 100 yards away. Approaching the fence, she made a hard left and leaned like a Harley Davidson, making tracks two or three feet below and on the other side of the fence that she managed not to crash through.

Junior's face was as white as snow when he got back to the starting area, and he vowed never to make that trip again. I ran a few steers on Miss Twist and, knowing her so well, I was able to catch them with very little difficulty. Meanwhile, John W. and Jack Roddy gave Junior a rough time.

It was about half an hour later when John convinced Junior to try a trip on Miss Twist one more time.

'You see how easy it is for Monty,' he said. 'Just jump. Don't ride by.'

Trying to keep his male pride intact, Junior once more backed Miss Twist into the starting box. After a second or so, he nodded his head and left in a similar fashion to the first time. As he passed the steer at full speed, he lowered himself about half the distance to the steer's back but it was too late and he found himself with nothing but that fence staring at him from the far end of the arena. He straightened himself in the saddle and, being the good Catholic that he was, made the sign of the cross and baled out. Junior tumbled for about twenty yards or so, scraping elbows and knees and blackening one eye, but he got up in a cloud of dust and said, 'I like that a lot better.' John W., Jack Roddy and I couldn't stop laughing for half an hour.

One time, the Cal Poly track coach invited an Olympic athlete to be the guest of honour at a meeting he was organizing. My rodeo coach, Bill Gibford, decided to match Miss Twist against the sprinter. I don't know what those

foot runners were thinking about but I rode Miss Twist, who was carrying 220 pounds of rider plus about 40 pounds of tack, and beat the Olympic sprinter by about 20 yards in a 50-yard race.

Miss Twist allowed me to win in bulldogging virtually every weekend throughout the 1956–57 rodeo season. I went to the national finals, once more held in Colorado Springs, in the June of 1957 and successfully completed my quest to be the National Intercollegiate Rodeo champion in bulldogging, for which I received the championship saddle and a silver and gold belt buckle. Miss Twist accompanied me into the arena and while most of my team-mates could not figure out how I ever learned to manage her blinding speed, they all realized she was the major difference between the rest of the bulldoggers and me.

This photo shows Miss Twist outrunning the haze horse – the left stirrup was snapped away so fast it is over her back. Note my hat has been left hanging well behind. We won this one in Pomeroy, Washington in 1955

UP PRINCE

By the fall of 1957, Pat and I had a six-month-old daughter, Deborah Gail. It was time to get down to the serious business of earning enough money to provide for a wife and family. We were living in an old railroad car that I had converted into basic living accommodation on a ranch near the Cal Poly campus. The arrangement included the use of modest horse facilities. If I remember correctly, I proposed that my fee for training a horse would be $125 per month, including food and stabling.

This was well before the time of disposable diapers and when Pat's mother, Marge, came to visit, she told me that our old-fashioned, wringer-style washing machine was just not adequate. An automatic machine would be far less work for Pat. Marge showed me an ad in the local newspaper – an automatic washing machine from Sears Roebuck Company would cost us $160. I could put $20 down and pay just $10 a month for two years. Off I went with the ad clipped from the paper.

I was directed to the credit department to have my contract drawn up but after I had filled out some forms, the lady behind the counter said I couldn't buy the machine because I had never bought anything on credit before. I had paid cash for everything, so I didn't have a credit rating. I would have to go home to Pat and her mother and tell them we'd have to carry on using that old wringer washer.

As I was about to leave the credit department, my tail firmly between my legs, I heard my name called out. 'Are you Monty Roberts?' a young man inquired. It turned out he was a cousin of mine. I had many relatives in the San Luis Obispo area because my mother's family had homesteaded near there. I noticed the young man had a Sears uniform on and he told me he was a maintenance man and also did deliveries. I mentioned my problem with the credit department and he ushered me back to the lady at the desk.

He told her I was a relative and I was good for my payments. She said that if he was so certain, he'd have no problem with co-signing the agreement and acting as guarantor – and that's what he did. I don't remember ever seeing him again.

Pat and I told everyone in the community that we were in the business of training horses and we settled down to wait and see what came our way. All I knew was that I had to keep paying for that washing machine.

I came back to the house one evening, tired from a long day, and Pat told me we had received a call from a lady in Baywood Park who had a horse she wanted us to train. As she had no trailer, Pat had volunteered us to collect. A time was arranged and off we went. We travelled west towards the Pacific Ocean. Baywood Park is a beautiful seaside community about fourteen miles west of San Luis Obispo. The directions led us down residential streets and eventually to the number of the house in question.

The houses in this community had about half an acre of land, which allowed each one to have a large garden at the back or, as in this case, a small field with a one-horse stable. We parked our car and two-horse trailer in front of the house and walked up the path. Suddenly, a large side door opened to reveal a two-car garage with everything in it but cars. There were rabbit hutches and nesting boxes. There was hay, grain, a saddle, halters and various assorted horse equipment.

Standing in the middle of the doorway was a friendly, middle-aged lady who could be described as a typical animal-loving kind of woman. She must have made more trips to the feed store than to the supermarket. Asking us to ignore the mess, she escorted us through the garage and out on to the lawn behind the house.

About twenty yards across the lawn we could see our new customer in his field. Prince was a three-year-old half Thoroughbred stallion, nearly 16 hands in height. He was a bright bay and appeared to be healthy and athletic. The lady said she had a job and just didn't have time to train Prince, and her husband didn't ride. Apparently, she'd raised her family and was now returning to riding after a long break. She'd ridden a lot as a youngster and she felt she would be fine if I could just give him one month of training.

As the three of us crossed the lawn, I suddenly noticed something too frightening for words. A one-wire fence was stretched very tight just about waist high to form the boundary between the lawn and the field and Prince was standing with one front foot outside the field and one front foot inside. The wire was between his legs, drawn up tight into his chest area. Virtually every horseman has experienced serious injuries to horses caused by wire fences. It was a chilling sight. Wire can act like the sharpest knife.

I took the lady's arm and reached out for Pat, too.

'Wait a minute,' I said. 'Stop. We've got a problem here. The horse is tangled in that fence.'

'Oh, no,' the lady said. 'He does that all the time. He's just waiting for my husband to come and feed him.'

I asked her, if he did this all the time, how the heck did they get him off the fence?

'No problem,' she replied, handing me a lead rope. 'You just snap this into the halter, back up to the end of the lead, lift both of your hands in the air and yell, UP PRINCE!'

I stared at her. What kind of circus was this? I looked over at Pat who simply buried her mouth in her hands and doubled over, fighting back laughter. Here I was, National Champion in Horsemastership 1950, National Champion in Team Roping 1956 and National Champion in Bulldogging 1957, and this lady was asking me to stand at the end of a lead rope, lift my arms and yell, 'Up Prince'.

Once again I looked over at Pat, who rolled her eyes and said, 'Monty, if it works, do it.' My inclination was to run like a rabbit, get in the car and drive home, but I had those payments to make. I couldn't let my cousin down when he'd been so nice as to guarantee I was credit-worthy.

I walked very slowly towards the big horse. 'Hello, boy,' I said, soothing him. He stood like a statue but didn't look too pleased at this total stranger interfering with his feed time. I had no idea which way he'd jump but I clipped the lead rope to the bottom ring on his halter, backed up to the end and looked over once more at Pat, who just shrugged as if to say, 'It's up to you.'

I thought, 'Well, in this instance, do as you're told and do it exactly as she said.' So I raised my two arms and yelled, 'UP PRINCE.'

Would you believe it, this horse – who had never seen me before in his life – stood straight on his hind legs, lifted himself off the fence and gently lowered his forefeet back into his field. It was incredible.

We loaded him into our trailer and headed home. I got my $125, Pat got to keep the washing machine, the mystery cousin was never called on to repay my debt, and Pat and I learned something from a three-year-old colt from Baywood Park, California.

Pat promised she'd never tell anybody about this embarrassing first challenge for a brand new horse trainer, but I believe it was just three days later when, over dinner with our best friends, John W. and JoAnn Jones, she spilled the whole story. Telling John W. a story like that was certain to get it more exposure than reporting it to the *New York Times*. From then on, if I was competing in a horse show or a rodeo, I'd often hear someone call out, 'UP PRINCE!'

I've always known that humility is a great virtue, but how much humility could one horse trainer bear?

MY BLUE HEAVEN

Some time during 1960 I got a telephone call from Joe Gray, a contractor from Santa Maria, California. Mr Gray's grey mare, My Blue Heaven, was causing him some problems. I already knew the horse because I had seen her in several shows ridden by each of Mr Gray's two daughters. It was clear to me that My Blue Heaven was becoming progressively more difficult to stop. When running at speed, coupled with the excitement of competition, she would lock her teeth on the bit and take the rider for a frightening trip. To stop immediately by sliding the two hind feet is one of the primary objectives of the Western horse, and it should be achieved with minimum pressure on the mouth. Obviously, something had gone wrong with My Blue Heaven.

Mr Gray told me that he was concerned for the safety of his daughters and he felt the only solution was to sell the horse. This was going to be a problem because, while the daughters were having trouble stopping her, they were still attached to the mare. Mr Gray told me that he and his family were going on a three-week vacation to Shasta Lake, California, and advised me that his daughters' horse should be sold before they returned. He said he'd take care of the trauma this would cause, and asked me to be on the lookout for a horse for each of his daughters that would be more effective in the show ring, and certainly less dangerous.

My Blue Heaven arrived the next day and with her came a note from Mr Gray. It repeated his instructions that this mare should be sold within the next three weeks, no matter what the price. Mr Gray would check with me when he returned, at which time he'd be prepared to assess horses I might have chosen for the girls.

I rode My Blue Heaven that same afternoon and was surprised at how good a mare she was. Her spins, figure of eights and cow work were world class. I decided to try a stop.

I went very gently, asking her to stop from a trot in order to get an idea of what was troubling her. I encountered immediate resistance to the bit. She resented it and reacted badly to any pressure on her mouth. I remembered that she'd been ridden in some very severe bits and pulled on heavily while attempting to make her slide.

My Blue Heaven, with me up, winning one of her many championships on the way to two reserve world titles in the Working Cow Horse division in 1960

The join-up technique was a dramatic way of communicating with a horse, no matter the age or circumstances, and so I tried My Blue Heaven in the round pen. Sure enough, it worked. A sense of trust began to build between us, layer on layer, session after session. I could let her know that I understood what she was saying to me. My round pen was out back and well out of sight, so I could go through this procedure without being observed. I was still very concerned about disbelief and scepticism.

Join-up with My Blue Heaven was as positive as I could ask for. I felt we were on the same wavelength. I wanted to change her mindset completely and develop a way of causing her to *want* to stop. It was, to all intents and purposes, like starting from the beginning.

I made sure I trained on the best of footing – not too hard, not too soft. At one end of my arena I had a wall around 8 feet high and 15 feet wide, made out of plywood and well braced. To begin with, I just trotted her around, so she'd be comfortable with this construction. Once she was used to it, I'd walk or trot her slowly up to the board and just before her nose touched it, I'd sit down in the saddle and press down in the stirrups, giving the command, 'Whoa.' I put no pressure on her mouth.

Maybe fifty times we trickled up to that wall in this manner, and at the first positive sign that she was reading my signals – the weight down in the saddle and stirrups, and the command – I quit. I dismounted and led her back to the stable, creating a feeling of reward.

The next day, at around the twentieth time, I asked her to stop 15 feet in front of the fence without any pressure on her mouth. Again, I got off, walked around and allowed her adrenaline to drop to a lower level, building an atmosphere of reward. On the third day, I asked for a little more, a little quicker.

It was a question of creating the desire in her to stop. Within a week her behaviour had changed. It seemed this beautiful grey Quarter Horse mare was learning how to have fun with her stops and no longer viewing them as a painful fight with the bit.

I was excited by her progress and towards the end of her second week, I decided to enter her in a forthcoming horse show. I was unable to reach Mr Gray to get permission to make this entry and there was a fee of about $50 to pay, so I covered it myself. Should My Blue Heaven put in a good performance, it was quite possible I would find a buyer at the competition.

With another week left for schooling, My Blue Heaven got better and better. She reached a point where I thought she might win a ribbon. First prize was a Jedlicka saddle plus some money, and while she couldn't be expected to win outright, that saddle was dangling there as the ultimate prize. At today's prices, it would probably be worth around $6,000 or $7,000.

There were close to twenty good horses in the competition and before the show I let it be known that My Blue Heaven was for sale. No one was interested.

My Blue Heaven's figure of eight with flying lead changes was virtually perfect. The next manoeuvre was the stop – the horse is required to gallop at top speed down the middle of the arena and come to a sliding stop at the far end. To this day I can remember the feeling of exhilaration that came over me as I felt her hind feet scrape the ground with that awesome sound of a good sliding stop. Her spins were fantastic and her overall score had her near the top of the heap.

With the cow work left to do, excitement, fear and trepidation all rolled into a big ball right in the middle of my stomach. If we drew a good cow, we stood a good chance of winning. My Blue Heaven's cattle score was outstanding and as we finished I recall looking towards the judge, Bill Gibford, my old rodeo coach. He was motionless, mouth agape. Mr Gibford had seen My Blue Heaven many times and he told me later that he never dreamed it possible for her to accomplish the level of work she turned in.

All the competitors rode to the centre of the arena and when our number was called to receive the first prize, my family and half the people there fell over in surprise. We made a victory lap around the arena with the new saddle up behind me, and it was one of the most gratifying moments of my young career. You can imagine how many people met me at the back gate to ask what the price of this mare was and could they take her home with them then and there. I was pleased to say that, under the circumstances, I couldn't personally agree to any sale.

The next day I drove to Santa Maria with the saddle in my car, having made arrangements with the lady who was in charge of the Gray household while they were on vacation, house-sitting for the plants and three or four dogs. I placed the saddle in the dining room with a note attached: 'Please be advised that My Blue Heaven won the Open Reined Cow Horse competition at the Alisal Guest Ranch show. This saddle was the trophy offered as first prize.

Should you still be interested in selling her, there are a lot of potential buyers out there, but I think we should discuss this matter further.'

The Grays arrived home approximately twenty-four hours after I delivered the saddle and called immediately. I'll remember that call forever. My Blue Heaven wasn't sold, which was just as well – she went on to enjoy many triumphs. Under my training, she was second for two years running in the World Championship Reined Cow Horse division.

My Blue Heaven helped put me on the map in professional competition. She reinforced what I already knew – force and demand are seldom the answer to achieving our goals with horses. She managed to get it through my head that if I could create an environment where her work was fun, she would be more effective.

My Blue Heaven stayed with the Grays until she died in the 1980s and she was buried on their property in Santa Maria. I was so fortunate to have this blue-grey mare in my life.

HEY SAM

In 1961 Pat and I were invited to dinner at the home of Robert Anderson and his wife, Frankie, on Oahu, Hawaii. I had been judging a horse show on the windward side of the island and the day had passed successfully in idyllic surroundings. An evening spent in the Andersons' beautiful home rounded off the day.

Mr Anderson told us about his two-year-old Thoroughbred colt, Hey Sam, and asked if we'd like to see him. Pat and I agreed we would, imagining a trip out to the stables. Instead, the doors opened and Hey Sam was brought inside the house, there and then. You can imagine our surprise and delight at having a horse come right into the dining room. His beautiful bay coat shone in the lights and his manners were impeccable, a measure of how gentle he was then.

It was agreed that Hey Sam would come to me for pre-track training in San Luis Obispo, which was very exciting. I had always wanted to become involved in different disciplines of equine competition, and if I could start this colt successfully, it might open the door to the world of Thoroughbred racing, a particularly long-held ambition.

Hey Sam was well prepared and once he was with us we could go to work right away. Join-up was as effective as always at starting a relationship of trust and good communication. He completed his pre-track training in six months without incident.

We selected a particular trainer at Hollywood Park, a major Thoroughbred racetrack in Inglewood, California, so that Hey Sam might proceed with his

"HEY SAM"
GOLDEN GATE FIELDS   4/19/65   DONALD ROSS UP
SCRUB 2nd (2nd)   SIX FURLONGS   1:11;3   POOL HALL BILL (3rd)
ROBERT A ANDERSON JR   OWNER   FARRELL W JONES   TRAINER

timed works but it wasn't long before I received a call from the trainer saying that they were having a problem with him. It seems that his daily exercise rider had fallen into the habit of stopping him at the same spot on the racetrack after each training session. This was where two gates led off the track to the stables, which were obscured behind a high hedge. Hey Sam quickly came to know he could go back to the stables from there and every time he approached the spot, he began to stop on his own and veer off towards the hedge.

Without the trainer present, the rider began to whip Hey Sam as punishment for this behaviour. Resentment set in and, instead of cooperating with the rider, the battle lines were drawn. Hey Sam became violent. Very soon the rider couldn't get him past this point. As the rider and this young horse approached the hedge, Hey Sam would bolt outwards and stop abruptly against the hedge, trembling, and then he'd kick and fight if the rider so much as moved the whip. The racing stewards banned Hey Sam from all California racecourses.

I went to Hollywood Park and saw this exhibition personally. Right there and then, I became an advocate for banning whips in racing. I've given demonstrations and made speeches around the world on how destructive the whip is. The idea of banning them is taking root in Scandinavia and, to an extent, in England and western Europe but the United States has essentially turned a deaf ear, even to any reduction in the use of them.

Watching Hey Sam, I was devastated. This was a gentle horse, a welcome guest in his owner's dining room back in Hawaii. I remembered the many horses from whom I'd learned that pain and pressure were never the answer. I took Hey Sam back to our farm and went to work to regain his respect. In secret, as always, I went back to the beginning and began to recreate a partnership of trust. We had many long sessions for about six months.

It's my belief that a horse is never born bad. Hey Sam had no evil in him. He was misunderstood and mishandled. Once I had finished work with him, I recommended he be sent back to Hollywood Park but this time to Farrell W. Jones, many times champion trainer. I rode him for Farrell the first time he went out on the track and as we came round the bend, that hedge loomed up. He went past without breaking stride or altering direction. He didn't even flinch.

Hey Sam's first race – what a day of joy

While the racing stewards were very concerned about Hey Sam, they seemed to be satisfied that my work on the farm had changed his behaviour to the extent they were inclined to give him another chance. Farrell targeted a race at Golden Gate Fields in northern California on 19 April 1965.

The day of the race turned out to be stormy and Hey Sam would have to run in a downpour. It seemed all elements were against us but he performed like a true champion and won. He ran the six furlongs in 1:11.03, winning by ten lengths and earning the right to be called a 'superior mudder' for the balance of his career. A photograph of the winner included Joe Perreira in a black topcoat. Joe was Sam's regular exercise rider and I remember him saying it was like riding the legendary Citation against the field.

Hey Sam went on to win fourteen races and earn over $100,000. He and I had our challenges but it seems we both met them and learned from the experiences. I felt such pride in his success and a true emotional connection with this very special horse. In addition, he became – as I had hoped he would right from the start – my entrée into the world of Thoroughbred racing, an industry that proved to be the mainstream of my career for the next forty years.

RONTEZA

In late 1959, Sheila Varian came to San Luis Obispo with a young Arab filly she called Ronteza. While Sheila was an accomplished rider, she called on me to help her work on her skills to train and show Western horses in competition. Sheila, in her mid-twenties, was already a breeder of Arab horses and had a strong reputation for producing champions. In subsequent years, she has gone on to be one of the most successful Arab breeders in the world.

Ronteza was in the early stages of training and Sheila felt it was time to start her with cattle. She was convinced that she had a champion working cow horse in this little bay mare. At the time, I had about twenty Quarter Horses in training and I would guess that ten or twelve of them were well into the cattle-working phase. Within ten days or so, Ronteza was passing my Quarter Horses like they were wearing hobbles. She learned more in a day than most of the others were learning in a week.

I told Sheila very early in this arrangement that she was not going to show this mare. Ronteza was just too talented for a young woman with limited experience in showing working cow horses. I explained that I thought this filly had a chance to go on to be a contender in world-class competition with all breeds although Arabs were not thought capable of accomplishing anything like this.

Sheila had quite another idea. At first, she ignored me when I insisted I should be the one to show the horse, but later she became adamant, telling me point blank that she and no one else would show Ronteza. It was simply not an option. At the time, I thought it a terrible shame that this talented young horse would remain unknown because of an inexperienced rider.

The cattle-working phase of Ronteza's training progressed unbelievably well and, with Sheila in the saddle, Ronteza won several major competitions the following summer in the hackamore division of the National Reined Cow Horse Association. I had to come to grips with the fact that, while I always preached to my students that they should never underestimate the potential of their horses, there I was underestimating the potential of my human student.

Watching Sheila show Ronteza the following year was an incredible source of pride for me, a double whammy if you will – two students winning in the same class. What a feeling! Sheila and Ronteza served notice on the world of Western competition that they were ready to take on all comers, even if the papers she carried did say 'Arab' and not 'Quarter Horse'.

In November of 1962, Sheila and Ronteza were entered in the National Championships to be held in the Cow Palace in San Francisco. This was the largest and most important competition of the National Reined Cow Horse Association – 15,000 to 20,000 spectators would be there every day. Sheila must have realized her chances of beating the world's best on a 14.2 hands full Arab mare were slight, but you wouldn't have known it to look at her. Sheila Varian beamed with confidence throughout all three phases of the competition, and when it was over, Ronteza was the National Champion.

All the big names of the day were in there, competing with her – Don Dodge, Ray Hackworth, Bobby Ingersoll, Ronnie Richards, Greg Ward and me. I think I was third on a big strong Quarter Horse, but a tiny, bay Arab mare ridden by a girl beat all of us.

The list of lessons taught me by Ronteza and Sheila Varian is as long as my arm. The popular belief that an Arab wasn't capable of winning in world-class reined cow horse competition was wrong. I doubted that a small filly lacking in the bulky muscle structure of a Quarter Horse would ever be able to stand the rigours of cow work. I was wrong. I thought a young woman with minimal experience could never beat all of us testosterone-fuelled professionals and I was wrong again. A picture of Sheila and Ronteza hangs on the wall at home. I still feel a sense of pride – always accompanied by a wry smile – to think back on her monumental achievement.

This photo shows Sheila Varian and Ronteza winning the Working Cow Horse Championship in 1968, at the Grand National Cow Palace, San Francisco

BARLET

Sometimes a horse comes along that's too troubled and mean to engage in
conversation. Barlet was a horse made mean by people.

A movie studio had hired an actor, Slim Pickens, to feature in a film for
Disney called 'The Horse with the Flying Tail', about a palomino jumping
horse. Barlet, a foal at the time, was used to depict the early years of the equine
star. Much of the footage was shot in the Salinas valley and I was on the set as
a stunt rider. I had known Slim since I was a child; he was like an uncle to me.

'Hey Monty, look at this!' Slim called to me. 'Isn't this the cutest foal you
have ever seen?' Slim was toying with a stick and the little palomino foal was
trying to nibble at it. 'Watch this,' he said. He tossed the stick and the foal
turned and ambled over to where it lay, picked it up in his teeth and brought
it back, like a retriever.

'Incredible,' I agreed.

'He's like a little puppy,' said Slim. 'Watch this as well.' He turned to the foal
and slapped his own chest, calling 'Hup, hup!' The foal jumped up and put his
front legs on Slim's shoulders.

'See?' said Slim. 'Ain't this going to be the brightest Walt Disney horse?'

While it did seem cute at the time, Barlet also thought it was fun to perform
the same tricks as a two-year-old, whether he was asked to or not.

Before he was ridden, his owner, Marten Clark, had been showing Barlet
throughout the western United States and he was virtually undefeated as a
halter horse. In this competition, the horse is judged for conformation. It has

nothing to do with riding or performance and is designed to determine which horse is the closest to the model for the breed. The competition is for anatomical excellence.

I next saw Barlet at the 1962 Quarter Horse National Championships held at the Cow Palace in San Francisco. He was in line to be National Champion. It was a virtual certainty but Marten Clark had him in a box stall with electrified wires surrounding the walls. Without them, Barlet would attack the walls when another horse or person passed nearby.

When I arrived, Marten had not been able to get Barlet out for two days. He made me an offer. If I could get Barlet out of the stall to the show ring and

Barlet winning his National Championship for Open Quarter Horse Stallions in 1963. I'm at his head with Charles Araujo presenting

win, I could have a half interest in him. Then I could take him back to San Luis Obispo and put him in training to ride and show.

As a National Champion, Barlet's value would be somewhere in the range of $35,000. While it was a challenge, I was convinced there was no horse that I couldn't handle. I opened the door of the box stall and was confronted with ears pinned back, teeth bared and the horse charging at the opening. I slammed the door as quickly as I could and stepped back to reassess the situation.

Don Dodge, a former instructor of mine, had shown me a device he called a 'come-along', which entailed winding and knotting a long rope around the horse's head in a halter-like fashion. This device provided far more control than a traditional halter. Now I went to my equipment bag and got the rope I needed. With a bit of luck, a lot of experience and a young body, I was able to get the come-along on Barlet without being injured. With the rope in place, I felt relatively confident that I could control him. Marten opened the door and I led Barlet out of the stall and into a training lane where the footing was good. As I began to work him with my rope, I could see an improvement in his level of respect.

The competition was the following day and, with a bit of ingenuity, I was able to make a show halter that approximated the effect of the come-along. I showed Barlet, he won his National Championship and Pat and I became half-owners of this beautiful horse. He came into training with us and was later successful in the hackamore division with me on his back.

Barlet, in his small way, looms quite large in the scheme of my education. I wouldn't be as capable with horses today if I hadn't had my experience with him.

FIDDLE D'OR

Fiddle D'Or was an attractive palomino foal, considered well bred for a Quarter Horse of his day. He was foaled in 1956 in Tulare, California, bred by Perry Cotton, who owned the dam and also had an interest in the sire, Bras D'Or. A couple of years before Fiddle D'Or was born, I met Homer Mitchell, who had purchased a property on which to retire near us in San Luis Obispo and wanted me to train some horses for him. Mr Mitchell, feeling that Fiddle had potential, purchased him as a weanling.

Fiddle was brought to me at two years of age and I started him using join-up in the round pen. I liked him and, despite having slightly straight hind legs, he showed a great deal of ability. He wasn't the brightest of horses but made that count to his advantage – he didn't fuss or worry too much. The task was there, you did it – that was his attitude. He was like a journeyman athlete, steady and a pleasure to work with. I began the process of schooling him to turn, stop and do figures of eight. I worked him on cattle because I felt he would be best suited to the reined cow horse division. Fiddle's cow work and his spins were his strongest points from very early on in his career.

With his slightly straight hind legs, sliding stops were not so easy for Fiddle, but he would try for you every working day. His flying lead changes were a testament to true athleticism and he remains one of the outstanding working cow horses where the figure of eight is concerned.

Fiddle D'Or was one of the very first Western horses to spin by locking his hind legs in place and pivoting around one hind foot, literally drilling a hole in the ground. He brought a new dimension to executing turns by getting lower to the ground rather than elevating his body as he spun. He was a forerunner of what you see today with the spins of the successful reining and working cow horses.

I began to show Fiddle as a four-year-old in 1960. We started at Clements, California, in May and by the first week in November he was the World Champion Hackamore Horse with the National Reined Cow Horse Association. He completed his first season without finishing lower than third and coming first about 80 per cent of the time. During this first season of competition we won at many of the nation's largest shows.

Being second two years in a row with My Blue Heaven had only added to my hunger for a world championship with a reined cow horse. While I had won a World Championship in the junior division and two National Championships in rodeo, this was my first World Championship in open professional competition with a reined cow horse. I was extra proud of this accomplishment because it seemed to establish me in the world of professional horse training.

I decided to keep Fiddle D'Or in the hackamore – that is, a bridle without a bit – for his fifth year. This was unusual because most horses are hard to keep responsive and light in the hackamore under heavy showing for prolonged periods of time. I was competing in about forty shows a season and it would be unprecedented if I could maintain Fiddle's record through 1961. I thought Fiddle might just do it because he loved his cattle work so much.

During the months of preparing Fiddle for his second year of competition, I remembered so clearly the lessons of Brownie and how he'd needed me to ease up on his schedule and allow him to have fun. Fiddle didn't need to practise our stops and spins. Working cattle was a joy for him and, if I kept him physically fit, working a cow three or four times a week was all he needed to give me winning performances at the weekends.

I suppose Fiddle more than any other horse taught me that work should be the only discipline and relaxation was the best reward. If he made a mistake on a cow, I would put pressure on him, asking him to recover control of the animal as rapidly as he could. On the other hand, when he was in full control and making difficult moves look easy, I would stop him afterwards, get off, stroke his head and let his adrenaline subside. Fiddle came to love this routine and I think it's the reason he won his second world championship in 1961.

Fiddle D'Or in winning form: here he is at the trophy presentation for one of his
world championship victories – World Champion Hackamore Horse, 1960 and 1961

Fiddle was awesome and he simply ruled the hackamore division of the National Reined Cow Horse Association for his final season. His win ratio was close to 90 per cent and he was never below third place. So far as I know, Fiddle is still the only horse in history ever to win the Hackamore Championship two years running. With the fierce competition of the modern day, it's not likely we'll see this wonderful individual's record broken.

SCOTTY

Harley May was one of the greatest all-round performers in the history of rodeo. While he worked every event that rodeo has to offer, bulldogging was his favourite as well as his most successful.

Harley told me that one of the prizes he was given for winning the All-Around Championship in a South Dakota rodeo some years previously was a dark chestnut foal. A friend had raised Scotty for him but he needed a lot of training. It turns out that the friend was Bob Scott, which is why he named the foal Scotty. I had gone to school with Bob and shown horses with him as well. Harley wanted me to train Scotty to compete in bulldogging.

Scotty arrived in late 1961. Although he was green, he would accept the saddle and rider and it was time for more advanced training. I always kept a few steers around the place because I loved to practise bulldogging, and I made time each day to work on Scotty's skills. The early procedures were designed to train Scotty to understand that he needed to run past the left side of the animal, allowing me to slide off his back and on to the steer's withers. As soon as my weight was on the steer, Scotty had to move forwards rapidly and slightly to the left, so that my feet could make contact with the ground without his interference. Within a month or two, Scotty was allowing me to catch cattle. He was quick to learn and I enjoyed teaching him the elements of reining and working a cow, so that he would have a good foundation, enjoy his work and be cooperative. Scotty was fun to work with and within six months or so I was recommending to John W. Jones that he try him out.

John W. was my travelling partner in rodeo then, and I would usually ride whatever horse John had at the time. While I had Scotty, John W. was riding a horse called Blue. I didn't like Blue as a rodeo horse – he would let you down just when you needed him the most. Blue didn't have the fire in his belly that Scotty had, and often just when you were catching a steer he would cut across, so that your feet hit the ground in front of the steer, which often caused a somersault. This is not a wonderful experience to go through and can, in fact, produce serious injury.

To illustrate this, let me tell you a story about something that happened to me one day during a practice session with John W. We had travelled about fifteen miles to a neighbour's ranch. This guy had some bulldogging steers that were going to waste and John and I agreed to give them some exercise. He had a wonderful arena and everything was perfect. Pat came with us to help with our practice.

When we arrived, we found a note pinned to the front door to the effect that our friend had had to go away for a meeting, but the steers were there and to make ourselves at home. We drove down to the arena, which was about 300 yards from the house, loaded the steers into the chute, warmed up our horses and got ready to go. As I recall, we had two horses with us – Blue to bulldog from and Dude to haze with. Dude's job was to keep the steer running straight so the bulldogger could catch hold of the horns without the steer ducking away.

John W. ran the first steer and did a good job with him. After a few minutes of allowing the horses to catch their breath, I backed Blue into the starting box, fully prepared to make my run. Pat, sitting on a seat provided on top of the chute, was in charge of opening the gate. She had to step on a pedal to release the latch and allow the steer the freedom to run into the arena.

I nodded my head to Pat and Blue stormed out of the box. He got me to the steer in good shape but just as I was catching hold of the horns, he made a right turn into the animal's path. My feet came down across the steer's centre axis, almost under Dude's feet on the far side. It was like thrusting a stick between the steer's front legs – except it was no stick, it was my legs. Down we went.

OVERLEAF *Scotty's first run for me, in the Grand National Rodeo, Cow Palace, San Francisco, 1962. Champion Harley May is the hazer. Scotty got me to this first steer like the champion he later became*

The steer pushed his face right into the sand and then did a somersault over the top of me. Now his head was on my left and his body was twisted around my right side with his tail touching the ground over to my left, where his head is. I was in a steer sandwich. I could hardly breathe and the steer couldn't seem to move at all.

Any well-meaning partner would jump off his horse, grab the steer's tail and pull, allowing the steer to regain his feet and releasing the bulldogger from the tangle. John W. was anything but a well-meaning partner! He rode Dude back towards me at a leisurely walk. I recall yelling at him to get the steer off me.

'Pat,' he responded. 'What do you want from him? What do you need? We got him where we want him now!'

I am not sure of the language I used for the next twenty seconds or so, but it wouldn't be fit for publication.

John W. eventually hauled the steer off me. Luckily, I was not injured and the steer was perfectly fine. What wasn't fine was my memory of how Blue cut me off. I told John W. that I had a young horse coming on that would be so much better than Blue, and that he simply had to look seriously at the prospect of retiring Blue and allowing Scotty to become our primary bulldogging horse.

The best I could do for the next few months was convince John W. to buy Scotty from Harley May with the idea that Harley could ride him without fee in the future. I was pleased that we had the ownership of Scotty, but not pleased with the fact that I couldn't convince John to take him to rodeos instead of Blue. As far as I was concerned, we had the wrong horse on the team.

All through 1962–63 John W. resisted my efforts to make the change. We had a race one day and Blue actually outran Scotty. It surprised me no end and further convinced John that Blue was the right horse for the job. Bulldogging is a timed event and acceleration is of critical importance.

I believe it was in November 1962 at the Cow Palace when I drew a good steer in the first round and Blue cut me off again. I was furious. To think that Scotty was 250 miles away and I was riding Blue made no sense, so I drove through the night to fetch Scotty for his first run in actual competition.

The Cow Palace was not the place you would normally start a green horse. It's the premier arena for Western competition and rodeo but Scotty allowed me to catch a steer in perfect shape, which should have proved to John W. that he was the horse to use.

It still didn't work. Scotty couldn't get on the right side of John W. and late in 1963 he sold Scotty to Walter Wyatt of Bakersfield, California. Walter kept him for a few months before selling him to Walt Linderman of Red Lodge, Montana. Walt was a nephew of the great Bill Linderman and was interested in putting together a bulldogging team. The normal arrangement was that if a bulldogger didn't own his horse, he paid one-eighth of his winnings to the owner with another eighth going to the hazer. Putting together a bulldogging team usually meant that one person owned both horses and so received a quarter of the earnings.

Walt hit the road in late 1964 with a good haze horse and Scotty. The record this horse created in the next twelve years was absolutely unbelievable. Scotty was responsible for two cowboys winning three world championships. Ironically enough, one of them was Harley May – world champion bulldogger in 1965. The other was Jack Roddy, who won on Scotty in 1966 and 1968. Walt won three runner-up titles, in 1966, '70 and '71.

The National Finals Rodeo accepts only the top fifteen bulldoggers each year and Scotty won five times, four consecutively, which was unheard of. Guess who won on him in 1965 and '68 – John W. Jones!

When Scotty reached fourteen years of age, in 1971, he became the favourite of many high school and college cowboys. Scotty enjoyed his work so much that I fancy, if he'd had his way, he'd have been out there running past steers all on his own. Horses are excited by competition work and, in the absence of force, they'll love it as much as people do.

At twenty years of age, Scotty went to live with the Yedder family, who agreed to keep him at pasture for the rest of his life. He'd never been sick and never been lame. He died of natural causes about five years later. If you've ever owned a horse, you'll know why I included Scotty in this book. I competed on him a limited number of times and personally won no championships on him, but his earnings for his riders ran into millions of dollars. His honesty and dedication to his craft were overwhelming. I am proud to have played a small part in giving Scotty his early training. He became the champion he deserved to be.

NIGHT MIST

Night Mist was with me at the same time as Scotty. They travelled together in the trailer countless times. I can just picture them side by side in that trailer decades ago and here they are again, side by side in this book.

Perry Cotton of Tulare, California, raised many good Quarter Horses during the 1940s, '50s and '60s, one of which was Midnight III, a blue roan stallion of Hancock breeding. When bred to Lucky Lady Tucker by Lucky Blanton, Midnight III produced a blue roan filly, later to be named Night Mist.

W.D. Dana had a horse operation at Healdsburg, located in the heart of northern California's wine country. Originally a New York businessman – at one time he owned the Empire State building – Mr Dana became interested in the tradition of the reined cow horses of the West, bought a property and hired one of the best Western trainers I have ever known, John Brazil. It was on his recommendation that Mr Dana bought Night Mist as a yearling.

John started Night Mist in late 1960 and showed her very lightly in 1962 with significant success.

Mr Dana passed away in 1963 and the following year his horse holdings in north California were auctioned. I was showing and unable to attend, so Pat represented us. We had already asked our friends John and Glory Bacon whether they would be interested in coming in with us to purchase Night Mist.

Night Mist: World Champion Open Working Cow Horse, 1964 and 1965.
Shown here at home on Flag Is Up after retirement

John Bacon and I had been friends since we went to Cal Poly together. We once raced our horses back to the hotel in Mexico where we were staying. We'd laid bets on who would get to the bar first and, rather than dismount, we rode our horses right into the hotel, across the foyer and up the stairs to the bar on the second floor. On the way back out again, John took a moment while riding down the staircase to build a loop and made a perfect throw over the head of a mannequin standing in front of the dress shop. He dragged this dummy off the pedestal and across the lobby and out of the hotel's main entrance, which almost caused an incoming guest to faint with surprise. She thought it was a real person being dragged away.

John came from a very wealthy industrial family and could ride well but had never been involved in competition. He could afford to put up a significant sum and I was prepared to maintain and train the mare as my side of the partnership. If I did my work well, I believed I had a chance of producing a world champion.

The Bacons agreed, Pat was successful at the auction and Night Mist came to us. This would be our first venture into the area of high-level show horses.

John Brazil had done a good job of building a foundation for her and within a few months I felt we were ready for open competition. She was a wonderful mare. Talented and willing, she would give you 100 per cent if you presented the challenges properly. Our children nicknamed her 'Nice Mist'. Curiously enough, the Bacons had three children, two girls and then a boy, just as we had.

Night Mist came along at a time when I wanted to concentrate on working with our Quarter Horse stallion, Johnny Tivio, whose story comes last in this book. I had been showing Johnny Tivio in both the cutting and working cow horse classes before Night Mist came along. This mare gave me the opportunity to enter Johnny Tivio in the cutting horse division only. Night Mist filled the bill for the working cow horse classes in a way no one could have dreamed possible.

An interesting situation occurred in our first competition together. An open reined cow horse has to be ridden holding the reins with one hand and with no fingers between the reins. Night Mist had somehow developed a tendency to move slightly to the left as she galloped the straight lines that are part of every reined cow horse pattern. This tendency was not apparent in practice but, with the tension of competition, it was definitely there.

I had always ridden my horses using my left hand – as most competitors do – but after we went home following that competition I reversed the process and began riding Night Mist holding the reins with my right hand. It was awkward at first but it didn't take long to see that Night Mist preferred it. In our second competition together she performed much better. I don't know to this day why she needed that change of hands. All I know is that it worked.

I showed Night Mist through the seasons of 1964 and '65 with high hopes. She accepted every lesson and maintained her world-class competitive edge throughout and was world champion in both seasons. I remember at one point Pat telling me we had just passed the thirty victories point in less than two years. She was never below third place.

I won the Grand National at the Cow Palace on Night Mist. As a team we won a saddle at Salinas and again in Santa Barbara in the same year, and in 1965 we made a successful swing through Arizona, New Mexico and Texas with wins in Phoenix, Albuquerque, Fort Worth, El Paso and Houston. The Western horsemen of New Mexico and Texas knew practically nothing about California reining horses, and they marvelled at her ability.

In 1966, as I completed my cow work for the championship class, I felt Night Mist stumble and almost fall. It was right at the end of our work and didn't affect my score. When I came back in for the trophy presentation, I noticed her pointing her left foreleg a little as we stood in line. Naturally, I was worried and I put a bandage on the knee that night with some poultice salve. When I returned to her stall in the morning, she was definitely lame at the walk. I got her home as quickly as I could and radiographs indicated a slight fracture of one of the carpal bones in the near, or left, knee.

Pat and I decided it was time to retire Night Mist. We bred her to Johnny Tivio early in 1967 and the result was a chestnut colt with some roan in his flanks. Pat named him Mr Tiv. He went on to win two world championships with the National Reined Cow Horse Association under a lady rider by the name of Jody Gearhart. Night Mist was given a green pasture and a loving family for the rest of her days. She died during the night in her peaceful green field and was buried in our horse graveyard. Her memorial stone reads, 'Night Mist 1958–1986. World Champion Reined Cow Horse. Winner of 31 consecutive classes. Owned by John Bacon and Monty Roberts'. Those are the bare facts. The emotions are impossible to describe.

SERGEANT

Memories that have been dormant for decades have been aroused during the writing of this book. Some take me back to deeply emotional times, to situations that brought joy or sadness, but when I remember Sergeant, it leaves me smiling at how comical my experience was with him.

'Do horses dream?' is a question that has been bandied about for generations. Every dog owner is certain that dogs dream, so why not horses, too?

I hadn't owned a decent horse for roping heels for several years. I was going to show Night Mist at Monterey, California, and Pat had encouraged me to enter the open roping there and the mixed team roping as well.

'I don't have a horse!' I objected, but she had already taken care of that. One of Pat's cousins, Bill Lambert, said he would provide us with horses to rope on. I asked what I was going ride in the open roping and she replied, 'Old Sergeant!' Sergeant had been a darn good heel horse in his day and was about seventeen or eighteen at the time of this event. I liked Sergeant. It was a good choice.

Jerry Matney brought our two roping horses from the Lambert Ranch to the Monterey County Fairgrounds, about thirty miles away. They had been used on the ranch and, while one had shoes on that were adequate, Sergeant's feet looked terrible. I asked Pat to make arrangements with the on-duty farrier to get some new shoes on him before the competition began the following day.

The farrier was Bill Whitney, an old friend who'd been our farrier for most of the post-war years on the Salinas Competition Grounds. Bill was quite old by this time, and he asked me if Sergeant was gentle. The horse had burrs in his mane and tail and his overall raunchy look suggested he might be a bit wild. I reassured Bill that I had roped on him dozens of times and there was no question that Sergeant was gentle. That was a given.

Bill suggested I should return in about an hour and a half. Pat and I called in at the horse show and rodeo office to go through the necessary check-in routine, had a hamburger and then moseyed back to collect Sergeant. As we walked up, we both realized that something was wrong. Bill's assistant was walking briskly to greet us and he had a disconcerting look about him. I guess his eyes were open just a little too wide and his shoulders seemed to be a bit stiff.

'Bill's gone to the doctor,' he said. 'Sergeant kicked him and they took him away in an ambulance.'

'What?' I replied. 'That's not possible. Sergeant's never kicked anybody in his life!'

The assistant told us that Sergeant had stood without incident while three shoes were easily fixed in place. In fact, he was so placid and calm it seemed like he'd fallen into a deep sleep while being shod. Then, when his leg was picked up for the last shoe, he suddenly exploded, blew hard through his nose, kicked out, pulled back and tried to run away all at the same time, and caught Bill on the leg. It was incomprehensible.

The assistant agreed to put on the last shoe and while he was doing it, Bill appeared. He had a slight limp and showed us that he was wearing a bandage under his jeans. We asked what he thought had happened. Fortunately, Bill had a big smile on his face.

'Monty, I disturbed that horse while he was dreaming about a lion,' he said. 'There's no doubt in my mind about it.'

Sergeant never made a move while the last shoe was nailed on, and Pat and I were able to rope. Bill Whitney was OK to continue his shoeing for the balance of the show.

I've had many dreams about horses – Pat has often been woken by an arm landing across her face when I dream of being bucked off. As a child, I often dreamed of riding into the mountains, hiding away, escaping. Then I would watch myself getting stuck in the wrong place – dreams of panic and pursuit.

But do horses dream? Who knows – I suppose the debate will continue until someone straps a machine on a horse that proves it one way or another. For me, I'd just like to continue thinking they do, but never knowing for sure.

JULIA'S DOLL

P at was never a competition rider as a youngster but she loved horses none the less. She rode in the Salinas while she was growing up and her grandfather had a horse called Poncho, who provided her with lasting memories. Then along came Julia's Doll.

We'd been married for around six years. We had three children and the eldest, Debbie, was riding. Pat was ready to get back in the saddle and maybe start competing.

It was November 1962 when Dr Stephen Jensen of Paicines, California, sent four Quarter Horse fillies to our San Luis Obispo training operation. He had a price on each of them and asked that we get them started under saddle and promote their sale. There were three decent fillies and he had priced them at around $1,500 each. They were well bred, easy to start, and I think we found homes for them in a short period of time.

The fourth filly was an absolute gem. Julia's Doll was by Poco Rey out of Spanishsprings Julia. She was nineteen months of age when she arrived and as pretty a filly as Mother Nature could create. Julia's Doll had the muscling of a world-class Quarter Horse but the elegance and femininity of an Egyptian Arab. She was trim and petite where appropriate, while strong and rugged where a Quarter Horse was meant to be.

She was one classy lady and it seemed to me that she was meant to be shown by a female. I told Pat that she'd better start honing her skills because we had a potential champion in our midst and she was crying out for a woman to show her.

Dr Jensen had put a price of $2,500 on Julia's Doll. I thought she was worth closer to $6–7,000. Today, Julia would command a price somewhere close to $100,000.

Pat tells me that she remembers seeing me ride Julia that first day in the arena, and that she was producing flying lead changes before knowing the rider's signals. Her coordination was such that it was simple for her to make changes without becoming disunited. This is a rare quality found in very few young horses.

However, Julia's Doll was not a reined cow horse. Running, sliding and working a dirty old cow were not what she was cut out to do. Julia's Doll was

Julia's Doll shown winning one of her many championships with
Pat in the saddle in 1966

the epitome of a Western pleasure horse. She moved with the cheetah's silken quality. Her temperament was one of complete cooperation. Congeniality was a byword for this filly.

Julia's Doll was shown in hand in the spring of 1963. Pat also entered her in a few Western pleasure classes under saddle. To experienced horsemen this may seem an outrageous claim, but the record is there that in May, with about six months of riding, Julia's Doll, as a two-year-old and ridden by Pat, won an open Western pleasure class in Danville, California. It was a sign of things to come.

For the next three years, Pat and Julia's Doll ruled the female halter division and reigned supreme over the Western pleasure classes of the western part of the United States. Julia's Doll earned a Register of Merit in Performance and Superior Halter as well as achieving the status of American Quarter Horse Association Champion in 1964. Her trophies for Grand Championships line a long shelf in my office to this day. She was not only a joy for Pat to train and show, but Julia's Doll found joy in it, too.

Julia's Doll raised fourteen foals after retirement from the show ring, producing some of the most important Quarter Horses of our time. She and her daughters produced literally hundreds of thousands of dollars' worth of young Quarter Horse prospects in their time. Julia's Doll and her progeny affected the Quarter Horse industry in countries beyond the United States, including Canada and Brazil.

She died in 1988 and is buried in our horse graveyard. Her headstone reads: 'Julia gave 27 years of pleasure and left an outstanding legacy through her produce.'

The strongest lesson Julia's Doll taught me is that a good trainer needs to bury his ego and respect the wishes of his equine student. Find the thing they want to do most and help them do it, even if it doesn't involve you personally. A selfish attitude in training horses will eventually come back to haunt you the same as it will in human relationships. Julia might have done well in open competition under me but I can't conceive of her doing nearly as well as she did with Pat.

BAHROONA

The dream of training Thoroughbred racehorses dominated my thoughts during every night's sleep throughout the early sixties. I had loved every minute of my experience with Hey Sam and felt I could contribute a great deal to racing. In my mind, Thoroughbred racehorses seemed to be calling out to me and I felt compelled to answer the challenge. I felt in my bones that the next stone in my necklace would be a racehorse; I just had to find him or her.

I had purchased a few Thoroughbreds for California owners during the early sixties, but limited funds had sent me to sales of lower-quality animals. I recall one owner sending me to a third-rate sale in Pomona, California, with the agreement that I could buy as many yearlings as I liked, so long as their conformation was near perfect and I stayed under $2,000.

Of course, there is no such thing as a cheap horse. Each and every one is of equal value in the most important ways and certainly should be treated as such. I was determined to avoid the trap fallen into by some racehorse trainers who placed bets on their own horses and deliberately altered what they did to improve their financial bottom line. I made a promise to myself that I would never bet on horses and I've stuck to it.

In 1964 I was approached by Hastings Harcourt of Santa Barbara, California, the son of the founder of Harcourt Brace Publishing and an unfortunate looking man. He had a bad skin condition and his face was pitted and marked. He wore thick spectacles, he was bulky – tall, but overweight and soft – and he was enormously wealthy. This was old world money. Families such as his had owned racehorses since the long distant past. He was well connected to other leading families, with blue-blood friends who met at the Turf Club and at the races. Mr Harcourt and his wife wanted not only to join in this world of high-level racing, but to triumph in it, with horses they owned.

I had trained a Western pleasure horse, Travel's Echo, for Mr Harcourt that was very successful during the 1964 show season. As a consequence, he suggested sending me to the 1965 Del Mar Thoroughbred yearling sale so that I might select a few prospects with the intention of racing them on southern California's premier tracks. He proposed a budget of $50,000 to buy three or four yearlings. Was I interested?

Can you imagine how I felt hearing I would have a budget of $50,000 after being limited to around $2,000 per horse in the past? It took a fraction of a second for me to answer that question. Yes, I was more than interested.

I went home and studied every book and magazine I could get my hands on. I tracked the results of horses I had liked from previous sales. I spent countless hours preparing myself to make an intelligent decision when the time came to raise my hand and spend Mr Harcourt's money.

Del Mar is a racetrack near San Diego and ever since Bing Crosby founded it in the 1930s it has remained the site of the premier Thoroughbred yearling sale for California breeders. In the mid sixties the average yearling price, as I recall, was around $20,000 to $30,000. Many of the horses running in California races came from the big sales in Kentucky, Florida and New York, with average prices significantly higher than Del Mar. We were still paying fairly low money but I was convinced I could find a winner.

Pat and I went to Del Mar in September 1965. I had a pulse rate that would have scared any doctor and carried a sales catalogue filled with notes of the research I had done. We walked the grounds at first, just getting acquainted with the sales procedures and locating the various consignors of horses that attracted our interest. Pat read out the records of sires and information about the quality of races won by sisters and brothers of the horses for sale. To say that I was well prepared was an understatement but as soon as I began to examine the yearlings I settled down. I realized that my most important asset was not so much my recently acquired knowledge of the catalogue – anyone could look up a pedigree – but my instinctive understanding of horses. That was my particular skill. Pat agreed – we were getting too technical with all the research. There wasn't one yearling there that could read a pedigree.

While standing on a particular spot that will be forever burned into my memory, I noticed a blood bay colt walk from right to left across my line of sight. He was about twenty yards from me, being taken from one barn to another. This colt immediately struck me and we followed him, turning at the end of the stable and walking about another twenty yards. As we approached the consignment that included this yearling, we stopped and stood back as he was led into his assigned stall. The handler removed the lead shank and closed a screen in front of him. It was the type of gate that allowed the horse to put his head out and I watched his reaction to the activity outside.

I was captivated by what I considered to be a very bright but calm individual who seemed in full control of the nervous energy that appeared to be present in his frame in vast quantities. The card on the outside of his stall informed us he was hip number 65 and by Poona II out of In Regards by With Regards. We asked to see him.

No fewer than three attendants began to scurry around with lead shanks, brushes, hoof picks and even a can of hoof dressing. Good God, where I had been buying horses up until now, you were lucky if they even found a halter to lead them out. I never asked Pat, but I suppose she felt strange as well, as we stood there like a couple of wealthy prospective buyers. It was an uncomfortable feeling and one that I must admit has not left me to this day.

The yearling was led out for us and I was blown away by the quality of his conformation. The triangle (which is illustrated on page 87) was so good it overwhelmed me. The shoulder and the hip complemented one another in a way that made his movement cat-like. Few horses I had ever seen were as coordinated. My pulse had shot up and I realized I was in danger of giving away how interested I was in him.

I decided, as the day went on, to spend a lot of time around that stable standing back and watching others view this yearling, assessing him to see how he fared with the tiring hours of inspection. His character stayed pure and he continued to impress me until the moment he entered the sales ring.

As I recall, the bidding started off at around the $2,000 to $3,000 level. I had spent a lot of time at horse and cattle auctions and, while I counted myself an experienced bidder, I just wasn't accustomed to spending large sums of money for one individual. I stayed out of the bidding until it slowed down at around $5,000. I whispered to Pat that I was willing to go to about $15,000 for what I perceived to be the best individual in the sale. I think my first bid was $5,500. Soon I was trading bids with one other buyer, but I registered the winning bid at $6,500.

I was worried by the low price. Was there something I didn't know? It didn't seem possible that others wouldn't pay more for him. Prior to hip number 65, several had sold in the $30,000 to $40,000 range for horses physically inferior.

I took the colt home and met Mr Harcourt within a day or so to show him off. His reaction was a bit negative. He said that he'd sent me to the sale to buy horses of high quality with a good chance of winning races at the major tracks of southern California. He'd expected to pay $15,000 to $20,000 dollars for each yearling. He was firmly of the opinion that the price of the yearling was likely to indicate how it would perform on the racecourse. I knew that genetics played a large role in the success or failure of racehorses and I asked him to trust me.

Without explaining join-up to Mr Harcourt, I said that I would like the chance to train this young horse using my particular methods. I felt I could turn him into a willing partner in racing to the best of his ability. Mr Harcourt really had no choice in the matter and although he was reluctant he was still hopeful – after all, I had succeeded with his show horse the previous year in dramatic fashion. Mrs Harcourt asked if the colt had a name and I explained that choosing a name was the privilege of the owner. Mr Harcourt suggested that his wife should select a name.

We discussed the colt's breeding. His sire, Poona II, was an Irish import that had exceptional ability as a sprinter. California was the stronghold of world-quality sprinters and many of our races were organized with this in mind. I explained that In Regards was a mare that possessed blinding speed but was unable to hold that speed for the classic distances. She was the winner of an internationally approved stakes race.

There are Formula One horses and then there are drag racers, and I explained that I expected this colt to be a drag racer. With that Mrs Harcourt said she had the perfect name for him.

'BAHROOOONA! Doesn't that sound like a dragster?' Mrs Harcourt asked. We agreed it did and he was registered as Bahroona, a name that stayed with him throughout his life.

Bahroona was a terrific student and went through seven to eight months of preparatory work without a negative moment. He was every bit the athlete that I had hoped he would be, and I sent him off to trainer Farrell Jones with great expectations. In the world of Thoroughbred racing, there are licensed trainers who remain at the racetracks and the daily training of the racehorses is done there. I never wanted to become a racetrack trainer. My lot in life was to prepare the horses for their careers.

The triangle, as drawn for me by the staff of the University of Zurich

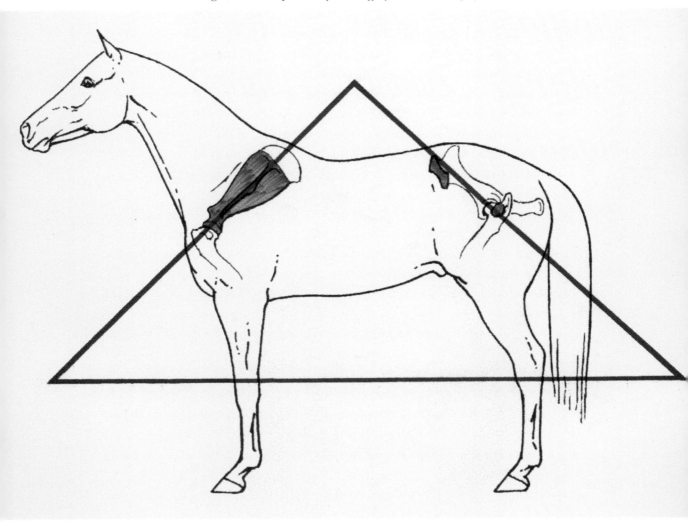

Farrell and I were having breakfast in the track kitchen at Hollywood Park one morning in early June. We were sitting with a group of trainers when Farrell and I agreed that we would target Bahroona for a race in July to prepare for a major internationally approved stakes race due to be run back at Del Mar on 10 September, almost exactly one year from the date of Bahroona's purchase. I remember one of the trainers saying, 'He's got to break his maiden [win his first race] before you start thinking about stakes races.' Farrell spoke up immediately.

'I think I've got a weapon here, at least for the sprints,' he said.

Farrell and I thought that the end of July at Hollywood Park would suit Bahroona for a first start. If he didn't perform in his maiden race well enough to win it, there would still be time to give him a second race before the stake. Bahroona's workouts were good, but Farrell was not the type of trainer to put undue pressure on young horses, so we couldn't know his maximum speed potential yet.

I got a call from Farrell about 15 July to say that Bahroona was entered for his maiden race on Sunday, 24 July. I told Farrell I was bulldogging and showing cutting and reined cow horses on that day in San Juan Bautista, California.

'I don't care what you're doing,' he said. 'This race is right for him and he's ready for it.'

I called Mr Harcourt and told him I had to see Bahroona's first race on video the following week because of my commitment.

'Not on your life,' he said. 'I'll send my plane to San Juan and fly you straight to Hollywood Park.'

I thought I'd be finished with my competition by about 1 p.m. and the race was scheduled to go off at around 5.30 p.m. He said he'd send a King Air, and we could probably get there in time.

I arrived at the Hawthorne Airport with a car and driver waiting and made it to the track in time to go to the saddling paddock about half an hour before the race. I sat up in the Harcourt box watching while they loaded the horses in the starting gate. The gates opened and twelve horses bolted out, each one straining to be in front.

They went into the first turn with Bahroona about two lengths in front of the field. He opened up ten lengths in the final 100 yards and won by the widest margin ever posted at Hollywood Park for a maiden victory. We were all overwhelmed with excitement. We dashed to the winner's circle and basked in this glorious triumph. I still have the photograph of us crowding around Bahroona, elated and surprised, our arms around one another's shoulders.

Bahroona rested through the month of August and then went on to win the Graduation Stakes at Del Mar by a margin of five lengths. He won $80,000 in two races, all within twelve months of that moment I first saw him walk by.

The success of Bahroona accelerated Mr Harcourt's interest in setting up a world-class Thoroughbred racehorse establishment. He had already sent me to Europe on a non-stop month-long tour to look at all the major racing establishments in England, Ireland, France and Germany. A private plane had been put at our disposal to cover the ground quicker. I came back with a plan in my head of exactly what I wanted, and I knew where it should be located. Mr Harcourt had agreed with my ideas and bought 1,200 acres of real estate in the Santa Ynez valley near Solvang, California. Within eighteen months he'd spent $3.6 million in creating Flag Is Up Farms, complete with breeding and foaling facility, a training and starting centre with stalls for eighty horses, a training track, two and a half miles of cross country gallops and a fully equipped hospital and rehabilitation centre.

On a hill overlooking the farm, a ranch house was built for Pat and me and our young family. It was designed in the early Californian style with extensive south-facing views over the valley.

My round pen was completely enclosed in heavy tongue-and-groove boards. No one could see in. Once I swung the heavy door shut behind me, no one would know what I was doing. I had become accustomed to keeping my secret. At some stage it would be right to show someone my concepts but not now. On the strength of one winner, I had been given the biggest break ever handed to a young trainer of horses, and I couldn't jeopardize it.

SHARIVARI

While Bahroona was winning the Graduation Stakes at Del Mar, the yearlings were arriving for the 1966 Del Mar Select Yearling Sale. As one might imagine, Mr Harcourt was flying high. Again and again, he asked Pat and me what we had seen in the stables that interested us. He wanted to repeat his success. It was some coincidence but Pat and I were standing not fifty yards from where we had first seen Bahroona when I caught a glimpse of a chestnut colt that blew me away. Was this possible – was this a magic place where perfectly conformed racehorses sprang out of the ground, right in front of my eyes? I held my breath and checked the catalogue.

Once again the pedigree was modest but the conformation of this horse would add a point or two to the overall score I had first given Bahroona the year before. He stood out like the glow of a gorgeous sunset, a copper red chestnut without a white hair on him.

Neither Pat nor I had this yearling on our list to inspect but I approached the stable of Dr Bart Baker, a respected California veterinarian, and asked him to show me this colt by What's Ahead out of Imbrosecco. Often a horse can catch your eye from a distance but, with close observation, you can change your mind, and that's exactly what happened. I thought he'd been outstanding from a distance – up close, I considered him to be the best I had ever seen to that time. This gorgeous yearling had a triangle that was symmetrical as well as extremely well proportioned. If Bahroona scored 9 out of 10 for conformation and movement, this colt scored 9.9.

There is no question that it is better to create the foundation of a racing operation with horses that have a chance to succeed at classic distances of a mile or more. The world of international racing has a tendency to minimize the importance of the pure sprinter and I thought that this yearling, unlike Bahroona, had the potential to produce strong racing ability over the classic distances.

In the world of buying horses, you learn to keep your opinions to yourself. You don't want excessive competition from other bidders, and there is a lot of work to do in the process of selection. You can't just like a horse and then buy him. If you're going to do a good job, you've got to study veterinary reports, X-rays and volumes of information about the performance of horses in your target's pedigree. The buyer who broadcasts his interests during the examination phase is generally less successful.

The fact is I was smitten with this yearling, but I didn't want to be premature with my comments. I knew that Mr Harcourt would get excited and try to affect my judgement, so Pat and I told him about the colt just before he went in the ring to be sold. While Harcourt was excited about my impression of the horse as a physical specimen, he was quite negative about the pedigree and went straight to his friends to ask their opinions. Their response was 'Are you crazy?!' I remember Mr Harcourt saying that What's Ahead was a failing sire and that Imbrosecco possessed only sprint capabilities.

Not to be denied, I went to the ring and bought the yearling of my dreams. When the hammer fell at $5,000, Mr Harcourt remarked, 'Well, here we go again.' If that were to be the case, it wasn't a bad deal. However, we wanted more than a Bahroona sprinter – we needed a horse capable of winning classic races if our operation was going to prove itself.

This yearling was among the first to be started on Flag Is Up Farms. We had transferred there straight away and the place was growing around us, but the round pen was built and I use it to this day. Around the first week in October 1966 the yearling and about eighty other Thoroughbreds arrived to begin their careers as professional athletes on our new Solvang property.

Sharivari was Mrs Harcourt's choice of name this time, and I know of no good reason except that she liked the sound of it.

It was apparent from the outset that I had my hands on something very special. Sharivari was athletic but, more than that, there was something between those ears that set him apart from all the rest. He learned his lessons with a brilliance

I hadn't known before, and soon went off to trainer Farrell Jones for his track work with a report from me saying that this was the best I had developed to date.

Farrell quickly reported back that he had the same feeling for Sharivari as I did. He advised us we should take our time with this one because we might very well have a classic horse. We gave him two races only in 1967 and they were late in the year. In the first one he finished third and it was an easy trip. Farrell remained excited and explained to me that this was part of the foundation building for this young horse and asked me not to be disappointed. Within a month, Sharivari competed for the second time. Pat and I watched as he dominated his competitors and won with ease, serving notice that he was ready to go. He'd be a classic three-year-old.

There was a gambling system in place in those days that enabled people to bet on the Kentucky Derby from January of the year in question. They called it the 'early book' and it was based in Tijuana, Mexico, because it was illegal to conduct such betting in California. When the early book was printed, Sharivari was the favourite for the Kentucky Derby, no less. My $5,000 yearling had been noticed.

The Santa Anita Derby is the West Coast stepping-stone to the Kentucky Derby and two races lead up to it – the San Jacinto and the Los Feliz. These are internationally approved stakes races run on one of the toughest racing circuits in the world. In 1968 Sharivari won both of them. He was now the favourite for the Santa Anita Derby as well as the Kentucky Derby.

About ten days before the Santa Anita Derby I received a call from Farrell. He asked me to come to Santa Anita as soon as possible. I was there at 5 a.m. the next morning and Farrell escorted me to Sharivari's stall. While the groom held him, Farrell showed me a tiny little bump on his left tendon.

Yes, your blood really can run cold. Mine did right then at the sight of that little growth on Sharivari's leg. Farrell brought in Dr Jack Robbins. I had known Jack for years and he was one of the very best racehorse veterinarians in the business. He was very clear and matter-of-fact.

'I can inject this small lesion with some cortisone and you might get through the Santa Anita Derby. What with the pressure of that race, though, I think you will not make it to Kentucky. Or we can stop racing him now and enter into a treatment programme and I think you have a chance he'll come back fighting fit next year, as a four-year-old.'

I was shocked. It took me five minutes or so to come to grips with reality. I was a professional and I knew that these things happened, but at that moment it seemed like the end of my world. I was totally drained.

The only option was to put the safety of the horse first. We stopped training immediately. Sharivari was given the best possible medical attention, with the idea of coming back about fourteen months later at Hollywood Park. The dream was broken but we still had a wonderful horse with credentials to be a sire. While injuries to the major flexor tendons on a racehorse are devastating, history shows that, with patience and diligent therapy, horses can return to win major races.

Sharivari came back as planned in 1969 at Hollywood Park. He was gorgeous and his legs looked as good as new. Once again, we all held out great hopes as he went to the starting gates for the Coronado Stakes. I watched him closely through my binoculars and he performed like a champion. About 200 yards from the finish, with Sharivari two lengths in front, the Harcourts were up and ready to go to the winner's circle. Then I noticed him falter slightly. He fought on gamely but finished third.

I went straight to the stable and remained with Sharivari through the cooling out process. He wasn't lame and you couldn't detect a visible problem. Pat went home and I stayed overnight. I was in Barn Three at about 5 a.m. and when the groom stripped off the night bandages, there it was. That pea-sized bump was back, just like we saw at Santa Anita the year before.

With Bahroona and Sharivari both back at Flag Is Up, I made a strong recommendation to Mr Harcourt that these horses be sent to New Zealand to become sires. While this was a far cry from the dreams of both Harcourt and myself, I believed that it was the best way to go for these incredible athletes. Bahroona was a pure sprinter with blinding speed in his family, and while Sharivari could hold his speed for the classic distance, he was genetically a sprinter as well. New Zealand was the Mecca for distance blood. The mares that would come to them were best at a mile and a half and up to two miles. It was my opinion that these two sires would put brilliance into New Zealand pedigrees and therefore be very popular. We made a trip and decided to lease a place called Alton Lodge near Te Kauwhata in the heart of horse country on North Island.

New Zealand had extreme quarantine requirements and after all arrangements were made, it was nearly a year before the pair arrived at the seaport in Auckland. We had secured the services of a New Zealand agent, Eric Hayden, to handle the business aspects of the breeding careers of our two stallions. Hayden was a wily character. He stood around five foot ten, was in his late fifties and had what I called an office body, that is he was not physically fit. He was a chain smoker, and he tilted up on his toes all the time, as if with that extra inch of height he could get more out of his cigarette. He dragged on it until it was burning his lip.

Sharivari and Bahroona were taken directly to Alton Lodge and settled in for a day or so before we got a call from Hayden. He said he liked Bahroona very much and believed he would be well received by the breeders for the 1970 breeding season in the southern hemisphere. He thought Bahroona possessed near-perfect conformation for their purposes, and he'd already begun an advertising programme for him.

As for Sharivari, Hayden thought he was the most beautiful horse he'd ever seen, with 100 per cent perfect conformation. He went on to say that his legs were OK and if there had been a bump on a tendon, it certainly wasn't there now. He said he had spoken with Mr Colin Jillings (a champion Thoroughbred trainer) about the possibility of training Sharivari to race in New Zealand.

'Are you crazy?' I said. 'We sent the horses there to breed. Don't even think of racing him.'

I explained to Mr Hayden that Sharivari had experienced tendon problems on two occasions, and that I had feelings for him like he was a member of our family. I didn't want to expose him to any potential further injury.

Mr Hayden was disappointed. A race was coming up, the Telegraph Handicap, that he thought Sharivari could win easily and, if he won, it would set him up to be one of the most exciting sire prospects in the country. I repeated my wishes to leave him at the stud and get his breeding career going.

About three weeks later the phone rang and it was Mr Hayden. He was shouting as loud as his lungs would let him.

'We won the Telegraph! Sharivari won by fifteen lengths. I've never seen anything like it!' I could just picture him, up and down on his toes, pinching the last inch of smoke out of that cigarette.

I was stunned, speechless. When the shouting subsided I said, 'If you want to remain in charge of this horse, get him back to that farm and get on with his breeding career!'

Mr Hayden said it was no problem; he'd have a full book of mares now. He was sorry but he'd just had to do it because the horse had looked so right in training. He promised me Sharivari would be back on the farm the next day.

About a month later, I got my next New Zealand call. Mr Hayden said that Sharivari was training very well and had a great chance to win the Railway Handicap on the last day of December, if we wanted to enter him. They'd kept him in training just to retain his fitness for breeding, but his legs and movement were so fantastic he wanted to give us the opportunity to try one more time. If Sharivari were to win, he'd be Sprinter of the Year for New Zealand and we could double the stud fee for the following year.

There was another option, the George Adams to be run on New Year's Day, and Mr Hayden said that this one was at a classic distance and, if I chose it, he'd be Horse of the Year and triple his stud fee. Mr Hayden was incorrigible.

Sharivari winning one of his major stakes at Santa Anita racecourse, California

I had the safety of the horse firmly in mind but felt I could approve the Railway, an easier sprint race. If we could be Sprinter of the Year, that was good enough. We agreed that Sharivari would be entered in the Railway and then go straight back to the farm, fully retired, to become – finally – a breeding stallion.

I received my next call on New Year's Eve, 1970, and there must have been a hundred people screaming over the line. Sharivari was a ten-length winner of the Railway and the Champion Sprinter of New Zealand. There were shouts of congratulations and, while it was difficult to understand some of the accents, I knew that Sharivari was a hero.

Mr Hayden told us how easy the race was and how wonderful Sharivari's legs looked. He even told me they were watching Sharivari eat his dinner right then, while they made the phone call, and he was an extremely happy horse.

'Wonderful,' I said. 'He'll be even happier when he sees a field of mares and the breeding shed on Alton Lodge stud.'

Eric Hayden probably had two or three cigarettes in his mouth at the same time when he said something I never dreamed would ever emerge from any horseman's mouth. He wanted to race Sharivari *the next day*, and not just in any old race but in the George Adams at the classic distance.

'NO! Not just no, but HELL NO!' I cried. 'That's not an option. Sharivari is to go to Alton Lodge and retire. Do not race this horse tomorrow!'

'OK,' said Eric. 'It's your horse, you call the shots.'

Twenty-four hours later I got my next telephone call – he won. An even bigger celebration was going on and Sharivari was Horse of the Year in New Zealand for the 1970 season.

I probably never was quite this perplexed. How can you want to choke a man and kiss him all at the same time? It was an incredible moment.

Sharivari finished sound and became a major sire throughout the southern hemisphere. Looking back, it becomes clear that veterinarians can be wrong and, obviously, I came to a wrong conclusion as well. I was most intent upon protecting the horse, and I suppose I might make that same mistake again. In this case, those legs of his were a lot better than any of us thought they were.

All this was thirty-four years ago, and if everything had stopped after Sharivari, I would still feel as though I'd been one of the most fortunate horsemen of all time to have such an incredible equine partner. Sharivari is buried in New Zealand but the memory of him follows me wherever I go.

GLADWIN
AND ALADANCER

In 1967, I was off to the major yearling sales of New York, Kentucky and Florida. It was time to get serious about the business of producing Thoroughbreds for high-level racing. I was happy with the results achieved so far, especially with Bahroona, but I was setting higher goals for the future of Flag Is Up Farms. I was looking for exceptional physical individuals with pedigrees likely to be accepted by international breeders when they retired from racing. I was looking for blue bloods.

Pat and I travelled to Saratoga, New York, in August to search through the Fasig Tipton select yearling sale, which had been held in Saratoga for decades. Just as we had done for the Del Mar sales, we spent a lot of time researching the individual offerings and had reams of statistics about their families. We were looking at yearlings fetching more than $100,000 for the first time in our career. I hoped that my instincts as a hands-on horseman wouldn't desert me just because we had made a journey of 3,000 miles and were in a different world altogether, where blue blood ran deep in the catalogue.

Mr and Mrs Harcourt flew in just before the sale began. Pat and I had been inspecting and studying for two or three days already. The Harcourts were there for the action. Pat and I were staying at the Holiday Inn in downtown Saratoga while the Harcourts were booked in at the Gideon Putnam, one of the original five-star hotels of upstate New York. Saratoga was, and still is, a spa destination but their high-class hotel, which, even then, cost hundreds of dollars per night, didn't offer a king-sized bed.

Mr Harcourt was about six foot four and was certainly accustomed to a king-sized bed, even though they weren't all that plentiful in the mid sixties. I contacted the manager of the hotel and asked if I could arrange for one. The manager told me it was out of the question and that it was the first time they had ever had such a request. I said I'd be getting back to him.

Meanwhile, Pat and I managed to get a good furniture store on the phone. They agreed to deliver a king-sized bed to the Gideon Putnam Hotel, and I made the arrangements. I called the hotel manager back and informed him of the situation. He was extremely insulted but allowed my plan to go ahead. The bed was duly delivered and the Harcourts arrived, unaware of the fuss. They settled in and were soon ready to be shown some of the yearlings.

You might wonder why I was so involved in seeing to the comfort of Mr Harcourt. Was I an errand boy, or was I a horseman? I was a country boy who had a chance to enter the world of international horsemanship. This required financial backing and Mr Harcourt seemed to be the only one prepared to provide it. I had noticed his tendency to run hot and cold. My attitude was if it took a king-sized bed to keep his mood right, we'd get one. I was a survivor.

All of the sales sessions were in the evening after the races, and the four of us met on the sales grounds at about eleven o'clock on the first morning of the auction. We went right down the book, showing the Harcourts the yearlings we thought were physically acceptable. After my first two years of selecting yearlings, Mr Harcourt was very excited about the prospect of me choosing Thoroughbreds from a genetic pool far superior to that available to me in the California sales.

My wish list was quickly pared down to a handful of yearlings, and soon Mr Harcourt realized that the one I really wanted was a bay colt by First Landing out of Dungaree. He was hip number 76 and bred by Mr and Mrs S.H. Rogers of Virginia. I told Mr Harcourt that this yearling was the first one I had inspected that measured up to the excellence of Sharivari.

First Landing was not a major international sire. Dungaree was from a good family but she had not performed well. Mr Harcourt was less than enthusiastic about the breeding but he was willing to go along with me where conformation was concerned. The pedigree was superior to Bahroona's and Sharivari's in a major way but, even so, was not what we had come here for.

Gladwin on a very special day in my career – the words on the picture tell the story

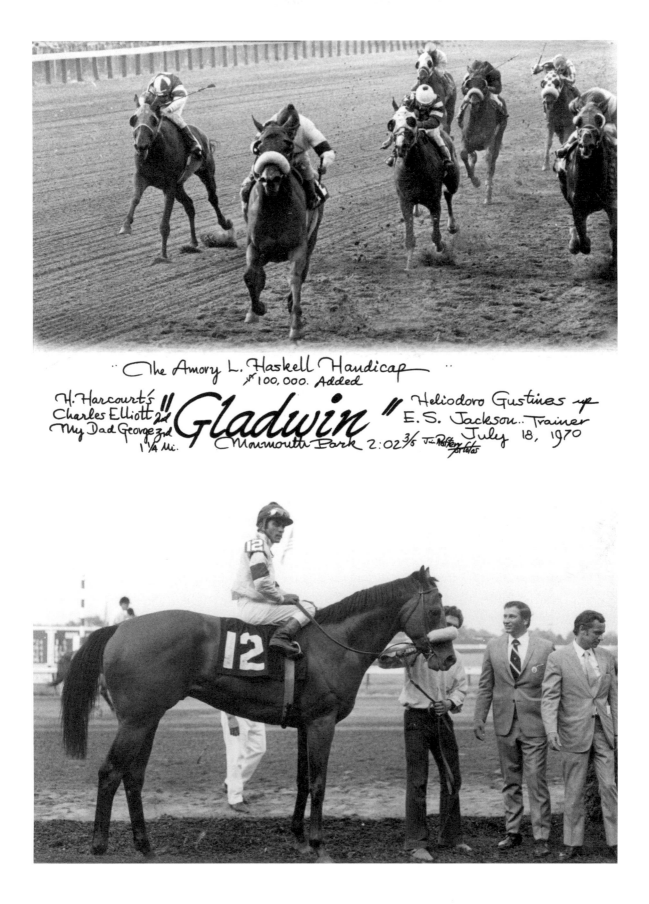

The Amory L. Haskell Handicap
$100,000. Added

H. Harcourt's
Charles Elliott 2nd
My Dad George 3rd
1¼ Mi.

Gladwin

Monmouth Park 2:02 ⅗

Heliodoro Gustines up
E.S. Jackson.. Trainer
July 18, 1970

We bought the bay colt that evening for around $30,000 and, while I was the happiest horseman in town, I don't think Mr Harcourt was too impressed. I remember he visited with many of his New York friends after the purchase and came back to me with words of advice from each of them – the First Landings were unsound and Dungaree was too weak a mare to produce a high-level racehorse.

Mrs Harcourt named this young horse Gladwin and he was one of the first of the eastern purchases to go into training on Flag Is Up Farms. I was determined to give Gladwin plenty of time and, despite an impatient owner, did not race him at two years of age. I put him in training in California with Farrell Jones and he had two starts as a three-year-old, finishing second in one of the races. Mr Harcourt had a long face at these results. We'd spent all this money and put a lot of work into this horse and it didn't seem as though much was going to happen with him. He was disappointed. Where was the glory in second place?

I thought that the hard tracks of California were stinging his legs and he needed the more forgiving surfaces of the east coast, so I suggested we try him there.

While in New York, I had made the acquaintance of a young trainer by the name of Evan Jackson. He was an ex-jump jockey, five feet six or so, wiry and nervous as a cat on hot coals. He was always walking and talking and turning around and walking and talking some more. He was outspoken and gave his opinions quickly and fiercely. He was also a workaholic and he knew the east coast racetracks like the back of his hand.

Evan Jackson, it seemed, was not only good with his horses, but had a very good female jockey, Robyn Smith, who was working with him in the morning and riding a few races. I knew her because it just so happened that she'd worked for us at Flag Is Up during our first year. I was a fan of this young lady; she rode well and, even more importantly, she had the ability to assess how a horse was performing.

Robyn fell in love with Gladwin and guided Evan and me into a training programme that seemed to put him on course to perform at a very high level.

Gladwin won a maiden race at Belmont as a four-year-old and, afterwards, Evan and Robyn both suggested that we should enter him in the Amory L. Haskell Handicap at Monmouth, New Jersey. I remember flying into New

York and getting a shuttle flight over to Monmouth. I rented a car and, following Evan's instructions, drove to Colts Neck, New Jersey, to pick him up at a private airport. Evan flew his own Cessna.

Evan jumped out of the plane and slammed the door.

'What the hell are we doing here anyway?' he railed at me. 'I got all the papers and tip sheets before flying over from Long Island and we are 65 to 1 on the morning line.'

Any bet on Gladwin would also get another two horses thrown in for free – that's what the experts thought of his chances.

Evan's news took me aback. All I could say was that we were there and we were entered, so we should just make the best of the day and take what comes. Evan repeated it was a mistake to enter him in a major race with a $100,000 purse. We should have chosen a lesser stake to test his wings among the big

Aladancer on the day of her victory in the California Oaks with me in a top coat

boys. I drove to the Monmouth Park Racetrack with Evan ranting at me all the way about how stupid his recommendation had been and I never should have gone along with it.

However, just like Bahroona and Sharivari, Gladwin couldn't read. He didn't know what a newspaper was and had never read a tip sheet. He'd never met a horse race betting expert, nor did he care what they thought. Gladwin entered the gate somewhere in the middle of the field, but finished the race approximately ten lengths in front of the second-placed horse.

There was no big celebration because Evan and I were there by ourselves and Evan was rather unhappy at having been so wrong earlier in assessing Gladwin's chances. However, I made a couple of phone calls home and I must tell you there was a tornado spinning inside me. It was a new high-water mark in my career with racehorses and one that will stick with me for the rest of my time.

Gladwin was four years old before winning his first race. During his two- and three-year-old seasons, a number of problems had cropped up, each of which had had to be dealt with patiently. I had learned to 'stay the course'. I believe that there is no such thing as good luck – it's simply a matter of being prepared to take an opportunity when it arises, and with Gladwin, that had taken a bit longer than usual.

We went on to race Gladwin in the Hawthorne Gold Cup in Chicago that same year. This time, the experts said Gladwin would never have the stamina to stay the mile and a quarter. They were certain his breeding wouldn't allow him to achieve that distance. Once more, however, Gladwin confounded the experts. He won the $100,000 Hawthorne Gold Cup, finishing his mile and a quarter in 1:58.8, a new track record. This would certainly set up my young stallion for a legitimate place in a breeding operation.

Pat and I went back to Saratoga in 1969, still in search of a true blue blood that had the kind of conformation I wanted and this time we found one – a filly called Aladancer. She was by the legendary Northern Dancer and she went on to be a major stakes winner, earning $191,135. She was a true blue blood with the physical ability to back it up.

As for Robyn Smith, she married one of the greatest entertainers of our time. She became Mrs Fred Astaire and was a loving partner for him for the rest of his life. Mrs Astaire has never lost her keen interest in horses and is often a visitor to major races throughout the United States.

MR RIGHT

Gladwin taught me a great deal about the ideal conformation of a Thoroughbred racehorse. He also gave me confidence to remain loyal to the impressions I formed in the early stages of examining and working with a young horse. He was also responsible for my acquaintance with Evan Jackson.

Shortly after I met Evan, Daniel Schwartz of Palm Springs, California, approached me and asked me to find a good horse for himself and a friend. That friend was Frank Sinatra.

They were interested in owning a horse that could perform in high-level racing and he advised me that, with his new partner, he simply couldn't take any chances. He said I had to look for a horse that was an established performer, as Mr Sinatra needed to have something to be excited about right from the outset if Danny was to keep him interested in the horse business.

I guess you could say I was motivated. I investigated leads from Florida to New York, out to Chicago and up and down the Pacific Coast. It was Evan who came to me one day and said I should consider purchasing Mr Right for Schwartz and Sinatra. Mr Right belonged to Peter Duchin, one of the most famous concert pianists of the time.

Mr Right was already a stakes winner and had proven his worth on both coasts before I came into the picture. I believe he had about $200,000 in race earnings and seemed to be sound and ready to continue his already successful career. The danger was that if under my management his performance tailed off, it wouldn't look good for me. Horses can lose interest in racing, even without bad management. It does happen, and I would be in the granddaddy of all fishbowls if it happened in this case.

Evan had been training Mr Right, so he knew him and, obviously, I was pleased to leave him there with the idea of racing in both New York and California. Mr Right was a relatively small horse but he answered my call in a very big way. He retired at the end of the 1969 season with seventeen wins and $667,193 in earnings, number eight on the list of all-time earners up until then.

Schwartz and Sinatra had a lot of fun with Mr Right. I helped syndicate him for them and he retired from racing to a successful breeding career.

During the process of selecting Mr Right, I learned a whole new discipline in my horsemanship. For the first time, I had to judge a racehorse that was already performing at a high level. I had to assess his soundness and decide on his potential to continue to race with enthusiasm.

I felt I had come a long, long way from riding Ginger and winning that trophy, aged four. It was a whole world away from rounding up mustangs on the ranges of Nevada and achieving join-up in the wild with Buster. My roots were in natural surroundings, not in the big cities, where racetracks were located. Mr Right introduced Pat and me to a world of high-profile people and showed us that horses could take us to places we never dreamed possible.

Mr Right helped to validate my theory that a horse is a horse. Their needs are similar, blue blood or mustang, and a good horseman should be able to judge their performance, whether ranch horse or blue-blood racer.

ROUGH FROLIC
AND CATHY HONEY

With Mr Right's success, there was palpable excitement in the Schwartz-Sinatra camp. Pat and I went to Palm Springs for a party that Frank threw to open a restaurant called Jilly's West. Jilly Rizzo was a life-long friend of Frank and had moved to Palm Springs from New York so they could continue their friendship without so much travel.

When Frank went out for dinner, it was a lot of fun. As you might imagine, there was a private room because it was difficult to enjoy an evening if the public had free access to him. I recall that about twenty of Frank's friends and relatives were invited on this particular evening. His daughter Tina and Frank Jr were there and his favourite piano player, Joey Bushkin, was at the keys. Frank sang a couple of funny little songs and seemed to be interested in getting others to perform. Dinah Shore took the mike, which was an incredible experience for me because I had been a life-long fan. Frank Jr sang some songs and got everyone laughing with stories about his dad and the family. It was an enchanted evening.

Frank went right around the table calling out the name of the next person to take the mike. He even had Jilly tell a few jokes and stories of the old days in New York and New Jersey before they had made their way to California. Dale Robertson was one of the guests that night, an actor with whom I had worked many years before. He was the star of 'Tales of Wells Fargo' on television during the 1950s. Dale was tall and handsome and before that evening I had no idea what a great voice he had.

Pat and I were sitting near the end of the table and, as Frank progressed towards us, I remember Danny calling out and saying, 'Sing us a few songs, Monty. What's your voice like?' Frank spoke up quickly and saved me the embarrassment by saying, 'You just keep producing horses like Mr Right and you don't have to sing for your supper.'

The evening finished up with everyone around the piano while Mr Bushkin played some of the most beautiful music I had ever heard. He was a true genius.

Pat and I were the houseguests of the Schwartzes that night and we accompanied them to Frank Sinatra's house the following day for brunch around the pool. Danny and Frank took me aside at one point and told me that now that Mr Right had retired, they would like to buy another racehorse. They didn't mind taking a bit of a chance this time, but they would like it if they could buy a two-year-old that showed some ability to run. I asked what sort of a price range they were thinking of, and they replied that price was not a concern; they wanted to shoot for a world-class performer.

In 1969, there was a new way of marketing young Thoroughbreds – two-year-olds in training sales. The horses had to be ridden under racetrack conditions. There was no requirement to exhibit work at speed, but often the consignors chose to go a sharp quarter of a mile or so in order to impress the buyers. These sales began in Florida and were usually held on one of the major racetracks in that state.

I discussed the upcoming catalogue with Frank and Danny and suggested there were approximately twenty high-class colts in the 1969 edition of the Florida breeders premier two-year-olds in training sale. Frank asked me to sharpen my eyes and go and find him the best young stallion on offer, both in terms of conformation and pedigree.

Once again, I was as motivated as anyone could be. Pat and I pored over the catalogue for the upcoming sale, which was to be conducted at the Hialeah Race Course, Miami, Florida. I travelled to Miami alone about a week before the sale proper in order to watch the training of the horses each morning before they were actually sold. I went to the track at about 5 a.m. each day so I could get to know as much as possible about the individuals that caught my eye. Many of my targets were eliminated within a three or four-minute inspection. I wanted near-perfect conformation.

A chestnut colt impressed me from the first moment I saw him. He was in the consignment of Ocala Stud Farms Incorporated. The colt was by Rough'n'Tumble, a leading Florida sire, and out of Individuality, a good mare from a high-class family. He was already named, Rough Frolic, and was one of the most impressive young Thoroughbreds I had examined up to that point in my career. I judged him to be right up there with Sharivari and Gladwin.

I called Frank and Danny and went over the page with them, explaining that I thought it possible that Rough Frolic would be the sales-topper. It appeared to me that many of the good horsemen there were paying a lot of attention to him. Schwartz and Sinatra both said that if I liked him that much, try to get him. 'What's my ceiling?' I asked. 'Half a million dollars,' they replied.

I tried to be calm during this conversation but when I hung up the phone, I did my best Irish jig. I was walking on air. Half a million dollars would have shattered all records paid for a two-year-old in training at that time. I was thirty-four, still quite green in my career, and here I was buying half-million-dollar babies for Frank Sinatra. I rushed back to the stable area with my sights locked on to Rough Frolic. I wanted to spend as much time as possible observing him throughout the daylight hours. I checked the veterinarian reports closely; they were as clean as could be.

While I was standing near the entrance to the racetrack, a chestnut filly walked by on her way to a morning workout. She caught my eye almost as intensely as Rough Frolic had done a couple of days before. Catalogue numbers were displayed on the horses' saddlecloths and I quickly opened my book to her page. Cathy Honey was her name and I saw she was by Francis S out of a mare called Honey Ration. By coincidence, Rough Frolic was coming from his stable at the same moment, and so I could watch both of them on the racetrack at the same time.

Cathy Honey was probably the smoothest travelling filly I had ever seen. She moved over the racecourse like a gazelle. She was elegant and feminine but, at the same time, her muscular frame had a ruggedness that promised an athletic strength few fillies possess. Her pedigree was mediocre but I had fallen in love with her. When she came off the racetrack, I followed her back to her stable to watch the cooling out session. I requested her vet reports and made my way to a pay phone in the barn area.

Rough Frolic receiving one of his many awards on the way to ruling the
Hunter Division of US horse shows in the early 1970s

My first call was to Danny Schwartz. I told him about this filly and said I needed more time to be certain she was everything I thought she was. I soon realized that I had disturbed Danny from a sound sleep – it was 7 a.m. in California. He had his catalogue on the nightstand beside the bed and when he found Cathy Honey's page, I can only think it must have been the early hour that caused his reply to be so abrupt.

'Forget about it!' he said. 'Are you crazy? You were sent to buy the best stallion prospect the sale had to offer, with sufficient quality to be accepted internationally as a sire if we are successful at the races. We told you we were willing to spend a half million dollars. Now you call me and recommend a filly that has a page that ought to sell for $10,000 or so. We're not interested in buying this sort of two-year-old.'

I don't think I said ten words during what was quite a long conversation. I apologized for waking him and told him I never meant Cathy Honey to be a replacement for the purchase of Rough Frolic. I was calling because I thought I might buy her in addition to the colt. She was quite possibly a similar kind of athlete to Sharivari and Bahroona. I asked him to forget the call and said I would get on with my work regarding Rough Frolic.

Yet I couldn't get this filly out of my mind. I called Mr Harcourt, my partner in Flag Is Up Farms, and outlined the situation to him. He also advised me to adjust my thinking, to become more aware of genetics and to take less account of the physical make-up of young Thoroughbreds. He said it was genetics that gave a horse the potential for breeding on an international level – but if I could buy the filly for less than $15,000, he'd be interested in owning her just for the fun of winning some races, if she could.

I didn't get any sleep that night. When I arrived at the sales ring, I realized that every major personality in the Thoroughbred world was there and ready to bid. Very few people knew me at that point and I spent my time outside the sales pavilion observing the horses being prepared for auction.

Rough Frolic was the first of my two targets. The early bidding was brisk and soon it was apparent he'd be the sales-topper. Arnold Winnick, a Florida trainer, was my stiffest competition as bids passed the $200,000 mark. We were bidding in $25,000 increments towards the end, and I was successful at $350,000. Just to give an idea of what excitement that caused, the entire sale averaged about $50,000 for each horse that year and when a two-year-old fetched anything over $100,000, it was serious. $350,000 was way off the scale.

Arrangements had been made for Frank and Danny to be near a phone. They were happy but considerably less exuberant than I was. They congratulated me and told me they had discussed the pedigree with many of their racing buddies and felt that Rough Frolic fitted the criteria they had in mind for their future in racing. I explained my plans for shipping him by plane to California and assured them that I would ride with Rough Frolic just to be safe.

The press swarmed over me, wanting interview after interview. Their interest was keen because this horse was the sales-topper and the price was a record for a two-year-old up to that point. They went crazy over the fact that Frank Sinatra was to be a partner in this beautiful individual, bred in Florida by the state's leading Thoroughbred breeding operation, Ocala Stud.

They kept me talking and, as the minutes ticked away, I began to worry that my filly would be working her way towards the sales ring while I was answering one question after another from people who couldn't know how important it was that Cathy Honey was due to be sold in just a short while. I pulled myself away from the pencils and tape recorders about five lots before her turn, and raced out to the walking ring about the time she was entering the staging area. She was a thing of beauty but practically no one was following her – unlike the throng that had chased Rough Frolic into the ring.

My experience at auctions told me not to show too obvious an interest in the filly. People now had their eyes on me and, while they were still trying to figure out who the heck I was, it just might stimulate an extra bid or two if I was seen to have an eye for this two-year-old daughter of Francis S. I looked at the other horses in the walking ring while measuring Cathy Honey out of the corner of my eye. She walked with a proud arrogance that spoke to me of championship quality.

Cathy Honey fetched just $12,500 and the sales ticket read, 'Purchased by Monty Roberts, agent for Hastings Harcourt and Flag Is Up Farms'.

I now had two horses to escort to California, and one can only dream of the kind of excitement that I felt arranging for the air shipment of what I thought must be my future champions. The travelling went without a glitch and, although I was exhausted when I arrived in Solvang, I kept Pat up for hours on end telling her about the experience.

Mr Harcourt came by the following day and seemed pleased with Cathy Honey. It was about two days before Danny and Frank flew to Santa Barbara where we met them for the drive to the farm. They were making one of their first trips in a new G2 private jet. Jilly Rizzo came along with them. Jilly had purchased a pair of Sicilian donkeys a few months before as a Christmas present for Frank, and I had agreed to keep them on our farm. Jilly seemed to be more interested in the donkeys than he was in Rough Frolic.

We drove straight to the stable and Rough Frolic was put on display for our three guests. Frank and Danny beamed with pride when they saw him. As we watched Rough Frolic, Frank told me that Danny had mentioned my early morning telephone conversation while they were travelling to Santa Barbara on the plane. He said that he'd read in *Racing Form* that I had purchased the chestnut filly, Cathy Honey, and he was interested in seeing her.

My blood turned to ice. I had no idea that Danny had not discussed the matter with Frank immediately after my phone call. I thought neither of them had the slightest interest in her. I tried to make light of the situation and agreed at once to show them Cathy Honey, a silly little purchase of $12,500.

Cathy Honey came from the stable as proud and beautiful as she was in Miami, but after all she was a filly and no match for the magnificence of the young chestnut stallion. Frank had his catalogue in hand and he put his finger on the page under the name Francis S.

'Do you know who her sire is named after?' he asked.

'I've no idea,' I replied. Then suddenly, without being prompted by Frank, the ice in my veins turned to permafrost. Francis S, *of course*.

I suppose if this sire had been called Francis *Albert* S, my feeble brain would have picked it up. Now I realized that this stallion, based in Florida, had been named after one of the greatest singers of all time, the man standing next to me – my new partner, Francis Albert Sinatra.

'It's a sign,' he said. 'It's meant to be. I want to buy this filly and if Danny doesn't want half of her, it doesn't matter. But I would very much like to have her.'

I explained that not only did Danny tell me to forget the purchase of Cathy Honey, but he also said she wasn't the type of individual they wanted anything to do with. I told him that after that telephone call, I had contacted Mr Harcourt who had agreed to buy the filly. She wasn't mine to sell; she belonged to Harcourt. Frank said that, of course, he understood my dilemma, but asked if I could convince Mr Harcourt to let him buy the filly.

We all made our way back to the house where Pat had a wonderful lunch prepared. We ate outside, from where we could overlook the farm and the Sicilian donkeys, running and playing in a paddock just below the house. It was an unforgettable day, a beautiful memory for Pat and me.

After driving them back to Santa Barbara airport, I called Mr Harcourt and he came up with a brilliant idea – he'd sell Cathy Honey to Sinatra, providing Sinatra would sell him a half interest in Rough Frolic. That was great for me – I was going to be involved with both of these horses no matter who owned them. However, when I made the call to Palm Springs, Frank said he wasn't willing to give up half of Rough Frolic and the matter was put to rest.

Prior to sale, Rough Frolic had been given two official breezes (speed drills); each of these sessions is logged in the books as three furlongs in 35.2. This was quite acceptable for a two-year-old in the early stages of training. A successful racehorse will eventually be required to better this by about a second, but there was plenty of time for improvement in our outstanding chestnut prospect.

Rough Frolic was trained on the Flag Is Up training track for about thirty days before we asked him for any speed. I told my rider to give him an easy three furlongs, to allow him to choose his own pace. I just wanted the horse to tell us what he wanted to do. Rough Frolic finished the three-furlong work in exactly the same time: 35.2.

We continued training on the farm for the next two or three months, allowing him easy regular works until his joints X-rayed as fully mature.

In the early autumn, we shipped him to Evan Jackson at Belmont, New York. Evan had seen Rough Frolic a few times but his first phone call to me was one of elation with how the young horse looked. Evan was excited with the prospect of training another horse for Sinatra and Schwartz, particularly in light of the fact that Rough Frolic was such a high-class individual. Evan wanted to take his time with this youngster and target the classic races as a three-year-old.

I suppose it was about ten days or so before I got a report from Evan on the first speed drill there in New York. Evan said he hadn't pushed the horse and he went an easy three furlongs and performed nicely, finishing the drill in 35.2. We laughed at this. Rough Frolic had now worked three furlongs about ten times and each of them was in 35.2. Evan told me that was just fine, no one should worry; he would improve.

A month or so later, Evan was becoming a little concerned. He said that no matter what he did, Rough Frolic seemed to stick at 35.2. He was a one-pace horse. He looked good doing it, but it wasn't good enough.

The next months would prove Evan right. Rough Frolic never won a race in his entire career. I can only imagine how disappointed Sinatra and Schwartz were. I know how disappointed I was. I was the one who'd selected him and managed every step of his career.

The question now was what could we do with this very expensive, highly bred, gorgeous individual, who moved like a champion but whose clock was stuck on 35.2?

My background had been the show ring, before entering the world of Thoroughbred racing, and I thought Rough Frolic had the potential to be a strip hunter. Strip jumping is a contest where the horse is judged on the style of jumping rather than on the height of the fence. At the conclusion of the jumping procedure, the horse is stripped of tack and shown in hand, and the judge awards marks for conformation.

Cathy Honey demonstrating why she was voted three-year-old champion filly of the USA in 1970

While this is not a discipline as famous as the Kentucky Derby, the horse-show world looks very favourably upon an exceptionally beautiful Thoroughbred strip hunter. The event requires athleticism and beauty, and Rough Frolic had a full measure of each of these qualities.

We put Rough Frolic into training as a hunter and he immediately showed an affinity for it. We were able to market him for around $200,000 to a California man who was prominent in hunter circles. Jay Lennon became his proud owner and Rough Frolic went on to be one of the best strip hunters the US has ever known. He won championship after championship, enjoying a career that lasted about ten years. Mr Lennon was offered as much as $500,000 for him but he had such an emotional connection with Rough Frolic he refused all offers.

Mr Lennon eventually bought a farm property about ten miles from Flag Is Up and Rough Frolic was retired there. I was able to see him many times afterwards and he remained a beautiful individual until well into his twenties.

Meanwhile, what happened to Cathy Honey?

Cathy Honey went into training with Farrell Jones at Hollywood Park in mid 1969 and, while Farrell liked her from the start, he had the distinct impression that she'd perform better in long distance races than in the typical California sprints. Farrell gave her a very easy two-year-old season, demanding very little from her in a few races only. She won one of her starts, coming from behind, which validated Farrell's opinion that quite possibly she was a filly wanting long races. She wintered well in preparation for the 1970 season.

At the 1970 Santa Anita meeting, Cathy Honey won the Santa Ysabel Stakes. Once more she came from behind and won with authority. She came out of her race sound and Farrell and I began to plan her future. We both agreed that she was better suited to east-coast racing and thought she had a chance in the Filly Triple Crown, which was run in New York.

We made arrangements to ship Cathy Honey east and contracted the jockey Laffit Pincay to ride her in the New York races. She went on to victory in the Acorn States at Aqueduct, the Vineland at Garden State, New Jersey, and the Ladies Handicap back at Aqueduct. In that same year, she finished second in the Coaching Club American Oaks, the Mother Goose Stakes at Belmont and the Santa Susanna Stakes at Santa Anita.

Cathy Honey won $196,146 in 1970 alone. This record placed her at the top of the three-year-old fillies competing in America during that year. Jimmy

Kilroe, senior racing secretary in the United States, voted her the champion three-year-old filly in the USA for 1970.

She had a very mediocre pedigree but nobody told her that her father didn't really make it as a top-class sire, and nobody said that her mother had failed to impress the world with her breeding. What Cathy Honey had, only God can give a horse. She had a heart full of generosity and a body to back it up. She took to speed training like a duck to water and became a champion.

She was the exact opposite of Rough Frolic. From the first day she went into training on Flag Is Up, I knew I had something very special on my hands. She always seemed to have another gear you could ask for.

At the conclusion of her career, Mr Harcourt decided to sell her because an offer came through for $350,000 – ironically, the very sum that Rough Frolic had been bought for – and he just couldn't turn it down. Cathy Honey was responsible for a gross income of approximately $628,000 for her owner.

Rough Frolic never saw Cathy Honey race but if he had, I'm sure he would have been impressed with her beauty and ability. Cathy Honey never saw Rough Frolic perform as a hunter but I think she would have been impressed by him, too. Pedigrees and price tags wouldn't have mattered to either one of these equine champions.

The lessons of Rough Frolic and Cathy Honey are so reminiscent of my work with the mustangs. It wasn't until I wrote these stories that I consciously knew the power of the lessons of Buster and the no-name mustang. Someone once said never judge a book by its cover. These two Thoroughbreds drove that lesson home to me in spades. In the case of Rough Frolic, I had to keep an open mind and search out the place he wanted to be. The talent was there. I simply needed to find the form it wanted to take.

FANCY HEELS

Mr Harcourt had always behaved erratically in our business dealings. He suffered from a manic-depressive condition, so Pat and I were always ready for something to go wrong. However, we could never have guessed how wrong. I have described this episode in greater detail in my first book, *The Man Who Listens to Horses*, but it's worth giving a short account of what happened here because it changed our lives dramatically.

In 1971, when I was thirty-six years old and we had already enjoyed some great successes together over a period of around seven years, Mr Harcourt advised me that he'd like me to meet his psychiatrist. His intention was that I should have a full understanding of his psychological problems because this might help me understand him better and our relationship would be more likely to continue. He repeated what he often said – that our family meant the world to him and he didn't want Flag Is Up to go wrong for any reason.

I agreed to the visit and during the consultation I was told that Mr Harcourt suffered from something called sandcastle syndrome. I'd never heard of it and didn't have a clue what it meant.

'If a child takes great pleasure from building a sandcastle on a beach,' the psychiatrist explained, 'that pleasure is only exceeded by the excitement of watching the sea come in and destroy it.' I felt dread, to the bottom of my boots. He went on, 'Mr Harcourt has a pathological compulsion to build something up and then to make sure it's destroyed.'

This was worse news than I could have imagined. What had I got my family into? Back at home, Pat and I looked out from our terrace. Flag Is Up Farms was spread out in the valley below us. It had everything that we could want – a training track, breeding barns, space for up to 500 horses, the covered round pens, accommodation for staff and its own equine hospital. Everything was working. With Mr Harcourt's help, we were on the way to gaining a world-class reputation. We had built one enormous sandcastle.

Sure enough, it happened. The tidal wave engulfed us. Hastings Harcourt turned up with a lawyer and said he wanted out. The lawyer was there to put this into effect in short order. I was in a hurry to get it over with, too – there was a decent chance any new owner would retain my services. Mr Harcourt left the room and the lawyer took over. My hopes were raised when terms were being discussed. Everything seemed fair. I had a 5 per cent ownership in the property and this was being respected.

Then came the bombshell. The lawyer said, 'And Mr Harcourt's riding horse, Travel's Echo, is to be shot. He wishes you personally to shoot him. Furthermore, he wants you personally to shoot his wife's driving ponies.'

Mrs Harcourt had bought a pair of driving ponies but had never used them. We had kept them in good shape at Flag Is Up.

He then ordered me to shoot two racehorses, Veiled Wonder and Cherokee Arrow. Neither had performed well enough for his liking.

We'd been telling ourselves to expect something but nothing like this – and it was to get much worse.

I went into a frenzy of activity. I wasn't going to shoot any horses. I made some calls to close friends and within hours I had 'sold' them, carefully logging the money into Flag Is Up accounts so that I couldn't be accused of theft. I agreed to repay everyone, so essentially I was buying the horses from Harcourt at their appraised value.

Things went well to begin with. Mr Harcourt didn't realize what I had done. A buyer for the farm was found and things were moving ahead but Mr Harcourt began to stall. Soon we came to realize that the path Mr Harcourt had chosen would become a lot rougher for us. He made aggressive moves in an attempt to destroy everything in sight. He discovered that I'd saved the horses and had me arrested for theft and thrown in jail. When I was freed, Mr Harcourt became even angrier. The farm, the horses, our very lives were in jeopardy. We were told a contract had been taken out on us. The children were sent into hiding while Pat and I moved to a nearby farm – I even rode into the hills and lived rough for a time. Meanwhile, Mr Harcourt was selling off Flag Is Up Farms in lots, as fast as he could.

We were away from home for over a year, during which litigation flew in every direction. At the conclusion of it all, an elderly judge pointed at me across the courtroom and said, 'I want to see that man smile.' I loved that judge. A settlement was reached whereby Mr Harcourt was obliged to sign over to us what remained of Flag Is Up Farms as compensation for his malicious prosecution. The property was significantly reduced but the core of it was still there and now we owned it. We could go home.

With the changed circumstances, massive adjustment and restructuring was necessary if Flag Is Up was going to get back on track. We didn't have deep pockets, nor did we have the backing of a wealthy partner. Pat and I went to work with more resolve than we had ever mustered in our young lives. The overheads were daunting.

It was 1972 and I had been out of show-ring competition for five years. After this crisis with Harcourt, I felt a strong temptation to go back to what I knew best and make another run at producing championship horses, particularly in the reining, cutting and cow-horse competitions. The risks were lower than with Thoroughbred racing and the chances of success higher. At the same time, it seemed foolish to waste the experience of selecting and training some of the best Thoroughbreds to race throughout the late sixties. I was at a crossroads and, as I have done so many times in my life, I waited for the horses to tell me which way to go.

Pat and I have raised forty-seven foster children. Some were with us for a short time only, some for many years, but forty-seven is the final count. One of the girls who spent a large portion of her growing-up years under our roof was Sue Sparrow. Sue met Dave Abel while she was living with us and they were married in 1968, taking up residence in Elko, Nevada, where Dave became a prominent appraiser of the large cattle operations of the Great Basin region of the western United States.

Through Sue and Dave I found a horse that I hoped would help us kick start the new Flag Is Up Farms. It proved to be only part of the answer, but the tyre had hit the road, whether we liked it or not.

I had been talking with Sue and Dave about going to the Elko Horse Show to look over a large contingent of reined cow horses. They compete there every year. These are ranch horses that work long hours each day, honing their skills in assisting their cowboys. They are fortunate to work in a natural setting without the necessity of training that is specifically geared for the show ring, which in fact often tends to make horses resent their job. The Elko competition often showcases wonderful equine athletes with good work ethics and cooperative attitudes. During the early part of my career, I saw many horses from this environment become very successful in the show rings of the western United States.

This time I soon spotted a horse that impressed me. He was tall, copper-red in colour and very athletic. He had an unattractive head but the body and coordination of a potential show horse. I learned that his name was Fancy Heels and I kept a close eye on him in the early competition. He looked like a classic mustang/Thoroughbred cross with a fair bit of feathering on his legs. He had an attitude about working cattle like a border collie has about herding sheep. A little effort, I thought, could turn him from a good working ranch horse into a top-calibre show horse.

Fancy Heels won one of the preliminary competitions on Saturday, which earned him a place in the championships on Sunday. If I was to buy him, I hoped to do so before any championship classes. If he won, that would be sure to elevate his price. Dave knew the owner and told me his name was Randy Bunch, a buckaroo (a ranch cowboy) who could always use the money. He located Randy and made the introduction.

'Sure, he's for sale,' said Randy. 'That's why I brought him to town. I didn't come here for the scenery, but I've got a good horse and I want some money for him.'

'How much?' I asked. Randy paused for a minute and then raised his head, looked me in the eye and said $3,500. I was very surprised, considering that to be a low figure, and immediately agreed to buy his horse. We shook hands and I wrote him a cheque. As I handed it over, I asked Randy if he was looking forward to showing the horse in the championship class the following day. Randy looked at me with a quizzical expression.

OVERLEAF *With John Weister up, Fancy Heels shows his ability to control cattle, 1976*

'You bought him,' he said. 'You show him.'

'Wait a minute,' I replied. 'I've never sat on the horse. I don't have any clothes or equipment. I can't show him tomorrow.'

Randy crooked a finger at me and said, 'Come with me. I want to show you something.'

We walked towards Fancy Heels' box stall and Randy ushered me inside. He raked back the bedding in one corner and picked up a half-empty bottle of Jim Beam whiskey. He held it high between us to let the light shine through.

'That's how much whiskey it took to get me through the preliminary classes. I don't intend to drink the rest of it to get through the championship. I came to town to sell him. I've sold him, and now I'm going back to the ranch. Good luck tomorrow.'

I looked at Dave and I'm sure my expression told him that I was pleading for help. He shrugged and said, 'That's the way these cowboys are and if you want a shot at the championship prize money, you'll have to show him.'

Dave offered to find me all the equipment I needed and tried to encourage me by saying he thought that I had a good chance in the championship class.

I rode Fancy Heels for an hour or so that evening just to get acquainted with him. After tacking up the following morning, I rode him again for about half an hour, which was just time enough to get his muscles warm and to discover that he could trot at nearly twenty miles an hour. There was simply no time to figure out where all the buttons were before it was time to compete.

While I was ill prepared to ride the horse properly, Fancy Heels and I won the herd-working phase of the three-part championship. The good score was encouraging but I knew that the herd work was his strength. We were acceptable in working a single cow down the fence, finishing second in that phase. Our dry work was the weak spot in our performance but, nevertheless, we were second in the championship.

The important thing was to get Fancy Heels home. I intended to improve him very rapidly and produce a horse for world-class competition in a short period of time.

After a week of training, I had gained a lot of respect for Randy Bunch. The changes that were necessary were going to be harder to effect than I realized. Fancy Heels was a seven-year-old with well-established work habits.

After a month, Fancy Heels was 10 per cent less effective than he had been at the Elko show. I remember sitting down one evening and telling myself that I was a major producer of racehorses and the trainer of several world champion working horses. I told myself that I could get this job done. I just had to increase my efforts.

After four months of training, I realized I had made several mistakes with Fancy Heels. I had told him to go at *my* speed and to learn at *my* rate. I had failed to respect the years of work that had gone into him already. I made a decision to spend the time to get him back where he was. If successful, I would attempt to market him to someone who could take advantage of his skills without expecting world-class performance in the show ring. While I bought him for the express purpose of showing in high-level competition, I just hadn't recognized his position; I hadn't listened to him in this matter.

It was a lot of fun to discard the notion of major competition and to work on this horse in the areas that he found most enjoyable. It seemed to me that an event just rising in popularity was the place for Fancy Heels. The competition was called team penning, which requires horses to work cattle very much like a ranching operation. Fancy Heels became one of the best team-penning horses ever and carried his new owner, John Weister, to many wins.

There is no such thing as failure. Failure is merely the point at which you have an opportunity to learn, and while I didn't reach the levels I wanted for Fancy Heels, he was able to teach me some valuable lessons. There's an old saying: 'Don't judge a man until you've walked a mile in his moccasins.' I walked a mile in Randy Bunch's moccasins and found that he'd done a very good job of optimizing Fancy Heels' potential. Horses will often humble the best of trainers and, with the future of Flag Is Up resting on my shoulders, I experienced a healthy dose of humility with Fancy Heels.

Obviously, we needed to discover a part of the horse business that we could afford. My experience with Fancy Heels was sobering. I simply could not keep my farm and family 'above water' with show horses as a primary income. Thanks to Fancy Heels, I put my thinking cap on and formulated a plan.

PETRONE AND HOLLINGSWORTH

Pat and I came to the conclusion that we had to get in gear and produce some Thoroughbreds worth their salt or we would never keep Flag Is Up Farms. We were running an operation with enormous overheads and needed cash flow – quickly. I could work with all the Fancy Heels and start all the mustangs the world had to offer, but that just wouldn't get the job done. Yet we could no longer afford to take the high risks associated with investing in the world of blue bloods. Furthermore, we simply didn't have the money to do it.

We decided to explore the possibility of buying Thoroughbred yearlings and selling them as two-year-olds in training. A yearling sale was coming up at Hollywood Park in October 1972 and a colt was entered – consigned by Hastings Harcourt of all people – whose sire was Petrone.

We knew this French-bred stallion well because we had nurtured his American racing, and later breeding, career. It's an interesting story. His owner was the actor Eddie Constantine, often called the French Humphrey Bogart although he was born and raised in the United States. Eddie enjoyed three decades of stardom in France and, when he was in his sixties, he bought Petrone, a dark brown stallion by Prince Taj out of Wild Miss by Wild Risk. Petrone was raced lightly as a two-year-old, registering one win and one third. In 1967, at the age of three, he had seven starts with one win, two seconds and one third. The following season, Eddie entered Petrone nine times and he won just two unimportant races. Eddie, slightly embarrassed by this mediocre performance, contacted Murty Brothers Agency in Lexington, Kentucky, with a view to transporting Petrone to the US for the purpose of selling him.

I was contacted by the Murtys in January of 1969 and asked to go to Santa Anita to inspect this recently turned four-year-old. What I saw was a tall, lean, well-conformed Thoroughbred with the classical look of a European distance runner.

Petrone stood about 16.2 hands and had a body frame that would impress any student of equine conformation. Nearly black, Petrone had a naturally frosted tail, a mixture of black and white hair that many would call salt and pepper. He moved with an elegant stride and appeared to have four very correct, sound legs. I read the veterinary reports and discovered that he had been given a clean bill of health.

Petrone was the type of horse that could cross with California sprint mares and bring to the offspring the ability to stay the classic distances of a mile to a mile and a half. With a price tag of $200,000 Petrone was an interesting prospect, but a bit risky. Before making an offer, I contacted friends of mine in France who told me that, in their opinions, Petrone favoured hard surfaces and races of a mile and a quarter or more. I recommended to Mr Harcourt that we should try to buy Petrone for around $150,000.

Our offer was accepted and Petrone was put into training with Robert Wheeler. We went to work on a programme to quicken his pace and a series of classic turf races of a mile and a quarter to two miles was targeted for him.

The San Luis Rey Handicap at Santa Anita was target number one in my little plan to have a Group I winner to stand at stud at Flag Is Up Farms. 'Group I' is the term used for the highest grade of internationally approved stake races, just a notch below the classics, such as the Prix de l'Arc de Triomphe. Petrone came in second, performing better than I had seen in his French videos. He ran with a bit more speed, closed well and was beaten by one length, appearing to need slightly more distance.

Our next Group I challenge was the San Juan Capistrano Invitational Handicap at a mile and three-quarters. Petrone was an easy winner and thus became the Champion Turf Horse of the Santa Anita meet for 1969. We had purchased him in January and by April we had a champion. I was filled with excitement and felt that there wasn't a horse in the world that could outrun Petrone on turf over a mile and a quarter.

Petrone wins the San Juan Capistrano, Santa Anita racecourse, California

The next goal we set for him was the Yankee Gold Cup Handicap at Suffolk Downs, near Boston. He ran with the utmost confidence but finished third in a large field after experiencing traffic trouble. I watched as the eastern jockeys built a trap for John Sellers, Petrone's regular jockey, and stopped him repeatedly as he tried to make his run in the last quarter of a mile. Those are the facts; I'm not trying to make excuses. I will always believe that Petrone was the best horse in the race.

The Group I Sunset Handicap at Hollywood Park in late July would be Petrone's final race. If he could win the Sunset at two miles, he would be the Champion Turf Horse for Hollywood Park and thus California for that year. This would send him off to stud in grand style. The best horses in America were there to compete for the $250,000 purse but I was once more filled with confidence. Petrone's workouts since the Yankee Gold Cup had been outstanding and I thought he was by far the best in the field.

This time John Sellers took great care to avoid any traffic problems. He held Petrone out wide on the course, which meant he had to run a greater distance than the horses closest to the rail but ensured him a clear path if he had the stamina to overtake the leaders in the final three or four hundred yards. Petrone cruised along, sitting about eighth of twelve runners until they were in the final turn. Then John Sellers let out a notch on the reins and Petrone came flying into the home stretch, passing horses as if they were standing still. He opened about ten lengths on the field and won with his jockey standing in the irons, wearing a smile you could see from a mile away. There was certainly no need for a whip except to wave it in the air in celebration as Petrone crossed the finish line. He completed the two miles in 3:18.00, which was a new American record for the distance.

As a teenager I had run races like that in my head while I mucked out the stalls, playing the role of the racing commentator, talking it out loud, bringing horses across the line ten lengths in front and calling it a new American record. This time it was real.

Petrone was retired and began his breeding career at Flag Is Up in 1970. Now one of his offspring was going to help us keep our home and our lives together.

The colt's mother was Princess Pet, one of my blue-blood purchases of whom I thought very highly. She had conformation that was among the very best of my female selections, and I was excited that we might have the chance to buy one of her babies. If we could make this purchase for less than $10,000, it was my belief that we just might get him working well enough to sell six months later in the two-year-old in training sale. If we got lucky, we might get as much as $20,000 for him. We'd have expenses, but there was the possibility of some reasonable net profit.

With all this in mind, we went off to the October yearling sale at Hollywood Park, aiming to buy the colt. His name was Hollingsworth.

Pat and I examined him with great care and diligence. This was the first time we had ventured into the world of Thoroughbred ownership all on our own and I must say it was daunting. We checked the veterinary reports and, with all our homework done, we gave the yearling very high marks as a racing prospect.

It was our intention to train Hollingsworth and prepare him for the Breeders Association two-year-old in training sale to be held at the same venue in

March 1973, six months ahead. When Hollingsworth entered the ring, I don't believe either of us held out much hope that we'd be able to buy him for less than $10,000 but we agreed that was our upper limit. The auctioneer began his chant to sell this beautiful Thoroughbred yearling.

When we got him for $3,500 we were like a couple of kids who had just won a raffle. $3,500! How could you buy a good Thoroughbred horse for $3,500? We thought he was worth at least $10,000. We were young and invincible. There wasn't one moment when we questioned the wisdom of the purchase.

I had been watching some of the other yearlings and, while I was not in love with any but Hollingsworth, I felt a son of Curragh King might be a good buy at $5,000 or $6,000, yet I bought this chestnut colt we called Country Rogue for $1,100. Now that's crazy. You cannot buy a racing prospect for $1,100 – but I did. With $4,600 invested in two horses, we went home to get our bones busy preparing them for their next trip through the auction ring in six months' time.

Pat rode Hollingsworth, and often our daughters Debbie, aged fifteen, and Laurel, thirteen, were pressed into service as exercise riders. Both young Thoroughbreds trained well through the winter and came up to the March sale in impressive fashion. We were not back in the blue-blood business but I felt we had a very good chance of coming out with a good profit and paying some bills.

Country Rogue was the first of our two to go under the gavel and when he walked out of the ring, the price board showed $9,200. I suppose there were some embarrassed Thoroughbred breeders around when Pat and I did a war dance, celebrating the fact that on the sale of just the one horse, we had made more than the money invested in both of these two babies. Hollingsworth would be our profit.

With Hollingsworth set to go into the ring, our pulse rates soared. I had asked him for three furlongs that day in an attempt to impress the bidders, and he had answered with a 34.1, which was the fastest time recorded by any sales horse. Hollingsworth entered the ring sporting a brilliant, glossy coat. My long years of preparing horses for the show ring had paid off. As the handler circled him, the bids quickly racked up – $10,000, $20,000, $30,000 … $39,500 was the final bid. After they picked me up off the floor, I took the lead shank and walked Hollingsworth back to the stables. We had just topped the sale. For two horses that had cost a total of $4,600, we received $48,700. Pat and I were in business on our own and we were doing OK.

The journalists came running to the barn and they were full of questions about how I had come to choose this particular horse. I don't remember what I told them, and they wouldn't know what I was talking about anyway. I liked his conformation and I loved his mother and his father. What more was there to say? The genetics and the conformation proved that he could run.

Not only did Hollingsworth and Country Rogue sell well, but they ran well, too. Country Rogue was a good winner in California. Hollingsworth was the first winner from the 1973 two-year-old in training sale and was the first stakes winner from that venue. He was also the first stakes winner that Pat and I produced on our own – and from our first attempt.

Hollingsworth gave us the courage of our convictions. Our enterprise made sense. Others saw it, too. Several people approached us, wanting to invest in future purchases we might select. A gentleman from the San Francisco Bay area by the name of Chuck Wilson offered to be our new financial backer. We could ride the tide upwards if we had good sales, but he was willing to take a large part of the financial risk if we didn't do so well. This would allow us to buy more yearlings and increase the size of our consignment, which would improve our chances of success.

Mr Wilson was a great inspiration to both Pat and me. He turned out to be not just a financial partner but also a good friend. He became more like a family member than a business associate. Chuck Wilson would prove to be the wind beneath our wings when Pat and I took off on a twenty-year career as leading two-year-old consignors in the world of Thoroughbred racing.

From a business standpoint, the lesson Hollingsworth taught me might possibly be the most important any horse ever provided. Hollingsworth said, 'If you think you can judge horseflesh, get some courage. Do it for yourself. Believe in your principles and work hard to maximize your potential.' Hollingsworth set us up in business and I will be forever grateful to him for that.

AN ACT

With the money from Hollingsworth and Country Rogue safely banked and our agreement with Chuck Wilson in place, Pat and I purchased eleven yearlings for marketing in March 1974. We invested $93,172 and received $280,200. We were the number one sales consignor and had the highest-selling individual at $65,000. When expenses were figured in, we returned 66 per cent per annum interest on a six-month investment. Everyone was happy.

The following March, we consigned thirteen horses that cost us $191,000 to buy and brought in $387,000. Our farm operation was growing and making increasing demands on our time, and so the following year Pat remained at Flag Is Up while I went off to Kentucky to restock for the season. For decades the Keeneland sales pavilion in Lexington had been the largest venue for Thoroughbred racing prospects worldwide. I signed for twelve yearlings, among them the last crop of the legendary Swaps. This stallion had died in 1975 and, since he was so popular in California, I invested heavily in four of his offspring.

One yearling I noticed went through the sales ring at Keeneland but did not reach his reserve price of $10,000. The colt belonged to Claiborne Farms, the leading breeding operation in America at that time. The founder, Bull Hancock, had died a couple of years earlier and his son Seth was now president and general manager of the huge operation near Lexington. Claiborne didn't often consign to the yearling sales but they had a group in this one. They raised many of the best horses racing has ever known, including Secretariat, but while sound, healthy horses were the strength of the Claiborne operation, marketing yearlings was not. Their consignment looked ill prepared when compared to the yearlings in show shape presented by experienced marketers.

This particular brown colt struck me as having great potential. He was tall, rangy and correct in his conformation but he looked awful. His hair was sunburned and he had less flesh than was desirable. I loved the way he moved and I had a strong feeling about his attitude and the look in his eye. It was early in the sale when he went through the ring and I just could not bring myself to buy a horse in that condition.

An Act triumphs in the Santa Anita Derby in 1976 – a pivotal day in my career. Pat, draped in the winner's wreath, and I are in the centre of the photo, surrounded by more than fifty An Act fans

AN ACT WINS THE SANTA ANITA DERBY
SANTA ANITA, MARCH 28, 1976   8th RACE   1 1/8 MILES, 1:48
OWNER: KATZ, BRUN & ROBERTS, ET AL   RONALD MC ANALLY, TR.
JOCKEY: LAFFIT PINCAY, JR.   PURSE: $150,000 GUARANTEED
2nd: Double Discount   3rd: Life's Hope

Standing out back where most of the professional buyers hung out, I remember being so tempted to bid for him but my arm just would not raise itself. One of the reasons why I couldn't make a bid was the image of Pat in my mind's eye. Pat was, and still is, a fan of pretty horses. This brown colt was not only not pretty; in his condition he was downright ugly. As the bidding progressed, it became increasingly clear that the colt was not going to make his reserve. He left the ring and went straight back to the Claiborne barn, unpurchased.

I made arrangements to have my twelve horses shipped to California and left Lexington to get home and prepare for their arrival. They were due to make the trip about ten days after the close of the sale and, as I flew home, I couldn't get the Claiborne colt out of my mind. I read his catalogue page over and over. He was by Pretense. Trained by Charlie Whittingham in California, Pretense had been very successful on the California racing scene. My intention would be to sell the yearling in California, so it would help if he was by a horse that was popular in that state, and it didn't hurt that the leading trainer of the time had guided the career of his sire.

What struck me most about the catalogue page, however, was that the dam, Durga, had produced two fillies that were currently racing and showing a lot of promise. They were both owned by one of the leading personalities in racing at the time, William Haggin Perry, and he was racing them in California. What had I done, I asked myself? A giant opportunity had leapt up in front of me and I had failed to put all of the pieces of the puzzle together.

When I got home, I explained the situation to Pat and, of course, she was concerned about the horse's condition. She questioned whether we could get him in shape by March and present him as an attractive package to potential buyers. In the end, though, Pat told me to trust my instincts and make the appropriate decision. I called Seth Hancock immediately.

'Ahhhh, some guy from Chicago called me and said he would give me $7,500 for him, and I believe I'm going to take it,' Seth Hancock said. I felt my heart sink. I told him that if anything went wrong with the offer I would like to be considered next in line to buy the colt. Seth said that was no problem and he would call me if the sale failed to go through.

For the next two or three days I walked around the farm stepping on my lower lip. This guy wouldn't fail to buy the colt. I was an idiot. You searched all year for a prospect like this and then you let him slip through your fingers, asleep at the switch.

Then Pat called me on the intercom at the training barn and said that Seth Hancock was on the phone. My heart was beating a mile a minute as I said, 'Hello, Seth. What's up?' Seth told me that the man from Chicago had decided not to buy the Pretense colt and if I wanted him for $7,500, I could have him. I tried to remain calm as I told him we would be sending a cheque that day, and I arranged for him to be included with my twelve original purchases.

When the yearlings arrived, Pat was stunned with the look of the Pretense colt, but she didn't make a federal case of it. Her position was that I had my work cut out and I had better get busy if I was going to produce a two-year-old we could be proud of come March. I told her that he was a fixer-upper. He had his Wednesday clothes on but when we sold him, we would have him dressed in his Sunday outfit.

'He's a fixer-upper all right,' she retorted. 'You've just got a lot of fixing to do.'

I decided to name him An Act – it's the dictionary definition of 'pretense'. There was another reason why it suited him, apart from his sire's name. He was an incredible handful and every day he challenged me with one act or another.

His training went well for the first month or so. Starting the babies in late September, it was often the first of December before I let them canter. I'm a firm believer in lots of trotting for young racing prospects before their bones are mature. When An Act began to canter, it was not a pretty sight. I was very happy with his trot throughout October and November, but his canter was like that of a horse completely out of sync.

By January, I was still worried, but his two half-sisters, Sarsar and Mama Kali, had moved well up the ladder in California racing and both were looking like top-notch prospects.

It was mid January before I asked An Act for any speed and then I stood stunned by what I saw. Even in his first work, it was evident that when he put his body in overdrive, everything began to operate at peak efficiency. He began to look the part, too. His coat was glossy, his muscles seemed to grow day by day and, whether it was my imagination or not, for racehorses speed is the most beautiful look of all. By the time we got to Hollywood Park in February, An Act was a grave responsibility for me; my palms were in a sweat because I realized that he was a very special individual. In addition, he knew it and he would constantly play up in such a way as to scare me to death. There was no malice in him; he was just a baby full of energy. Champion jockey Laffit Pincay made the trip to Hollywood Park from Santa Anita one morning to give An Act his workout, and he was full of praise for my brown colt.

The bloodstock agents began to appear and I was offered $50,000 and then $60,000, but we were entered in the sale and I was determined to let the public set his value. The day before the sale there was a preview of all individuals on the track and I decided to allow An Act to breeze three furlongs with my regular rider, Hector Valadez, in the saddle. An Act and Hector completed the three furlongs in 34.0, a new record for a sale of two-year-olds.

The agents followed my colt back to the barn and I turned down $80,000 from a bloodstock dealer called Albert Yank. He was known as Alberto Pie The Good Guy, a dyed-in-the-wool horse dealer. His motto was, 'I'll stand on my head, till my ears turn red, to sell you a horse.' It was a good sign that someone so sharp was prepared to offer such a high figure to try to stop An Act from going into the sale ring.

Our other two-year-olds had done well in the preview workout, but as you may imagine, Pat and I were intensely focused on An Act. At six the following morning, An Act's groom, John Flowers, took him out of the stall for a thirty-minute walk on the lead. He was jumping through his skin the day after his first serious work and, through no fault of John's, he got loose while I was watching him. He ran like the wind, circling barn number three at Hollywood Park. I went in the opposite direction and met him around the back of the stable. He ran up to me with his tail straight in the air and blowing through his nose. I took the lead and got him back to John for twenty minutes more of walking. This time we kept him in the shed row where he felt more contained. It was a fright beyond belief, but he didn't get a scratch.

That night he looked beautiful as he entered the ring. The three furlongs he had run the day before proved his athletic ability. Somebody opened the bidding at $50,000 and it sailed by $75,000. The offers slowed down after $80,000, and the auctioneer went in increments of $2,000 all the way up to $100,000. I can still feel the excitement as I recall the moment he was sold. The price was a new record for California two-year-olds.

Albert Yank bought him after all. He'd put together a group of clients to form a small partnership to buy the horse. As if obsessed with paying $80,000, Mr Yank asked me if I really thought he was worth the $100,000. I answered him in the affirmative and with that he said, 'If you're so sure, take twenty thousand dollars off and you'll own twenty per cent of him.' I said yes.

I suggested to Mr Yank that if I was to own 20 per cent of this colt, I should be his racing manager. I wanted to make the decisions about his career if I was to invest to that extent. Mr Yank agreed and An Act came home with us to prepare for autumn racing.

We decided to send him to trainer Ron McAnally in September with the idea of racing him at the Oak Tree meeting at Santa Anita in October. I made everyone promise that this would be a schooling race and, regardless of the outcome, we would not ask for another outing until he was three.

Laffit Pincay was booked to ride An Act and I was as nervous as I have ever been in my life as I followed him from the stable to the receiving barn. He was like a playful puppy and I was scared to death that something might happen to him before we got him saddled. As we left the receiving barn to go through to the saddling paddock, An Act jumped and played and struck out over the lead. Getting loose from his handler, he ran across the lawn near the walking ring right through the throngs of racing fans. Visions of him when he was loose just before the sale rose before my eyes.

After jumping two park benches, An Act made a U turn and came running back in my direction. He actually came to a sliding stop right in front of me and I caught the shank, leading him the rest of the way to the saddling paddock myself. There are few circumstances in my career that frighten me more than this but it was almost better to do it. I could quieten my nerves with activity.

An Act was the perfect student going to the starting gate. He broke well and won his first start by about twelve lengths. His time was outstanding for a maiden starter. There was no question that we had an exceptional young horse on our hands and I began to plan for his 1976 racing season. I scheduled one more non-stake allowance race for January and then looked at the races leading up to the Group I Santa Anita Derby, deciding on a path often taken by Derby prospects – the Santa Catalina Stakes in March followed by the Derby in the first week of April.

An Act won both races. Obviously, we had great hopes for the Kentucky Derby a month later but it just wasn't to be. An Act developed a viral throat infection a week or so after the Santa Anita Derby and the organism attacked his left retinoid – a flap that closes the opening to the lungs when a horse swallows. He recovered but he'd never have the same ability to breathe. His racing career was over.

I was devastated. There was a world-class performer inside this young horse but we wouldn't see his full potential. In many ways, I felt very little responsibility for his achievements. All I did was help him to love racing and do it because he wanted to, not because he was forced to.

However, we had our Group I winning racehorse, and with earnings of $212,950 we looked forward to his career at stud. He was syndicated for breeding at a value of $600,000.

If Hollingsworth opened the door to the world of buying Thoroughbred yearlings to sell at two years of age, An Act escorted us through. For a $7,500 yearling to reach the level of a world-class Derby winner was unheard of in the mid seventies. An Act did it in grand style.

ALLEGED

Approximately six months after we sold An Act, I returned to the Keeneland sales pavilion for the 1975 presentation of yearlings. I was very confident that An Act, who by then was two, would be a superstar but confidence, by its very nature, is fragile in the racing business. I needed to find horses selling well below what I perceived to be their fair market value in order to make a profit on them in just six months. Low prices were sometimes achievable because horses were not properly prepared, or if a snowstorm blew up, keeping the buyers away, but the best consignors in the world were conditioning these yearlings, and since it was early September in Kentucky, we were not likely to have the snow.

Pat and I met with our investors before I left California and we agreed that, while we should move our sights a little higher, we had to keep our average cost well below $15,000. In order to accomplish this, we concluded that we should not pay more than $30,000 for any one individual.

Pat stayed in California while I made the trip to examine the horses and visit potential buyers. After making my initial round of the consignments, I was convinced that the average sale's price would probably be around $60,000 and it was going to be very difficult to find acceptable yearlings within our budget.

I spent a significant amount of time around the consignment of Lee Eaton. Lee was a friend of ours and a consistent producer of high-quality yearlings at both the Kentucky and New York sales. While watching his yearlings being shown to prospective buyers, a colt caught my attention, not because he looked well but because he looked awful.

Scanning his catalogue page, I found he was by Hoist the Flag out of Princess Pout by Prince John, which was world-class parentage. I noted his present owner was one of the most prominent breeders in the United States, Mrs June McKnight. I asked Lee about the colt and he said he was doing the best he could to present him for Mrs McKnight but that he had had a lot of problems getting him to the sale. Lee explained to me that the colt had been very ill with an infected navel hernia. Surgery had corrected the condition but his recovery had cost him dearly in terms of body condition.

I had gone through a somewhat similar situation with An Act, but the shape of this individual made An Act look like a subject for an oil painting. The colt was probably 175 to 200 pounds underweight and every rib was clearly visible. His hair was turned inside out and was dull as could be.

However, I was immediately struck by the fact that this yearling had a triangle that was desirable in the extreme. Its base was as long as I had ever seen and its symmetry was perfection, which was not difficult to see because every bone was discernible.

Could I buy this colt, take him back to California and let Pat see him? She hadn't made a big deal out of the condition of An Act the year before, but this time there'd be a strong enough cause for justifiable homicide. I put a low score on the page of this Hoist the Flag yearling but I wrote that he had the best triangle I had ever come across. I also wrote that I wasn't sure how valid the triangle was because I had no experience at judging one so visible due to ill health. I put him aside and went about my business.

As I recall, I purchased six horses and arranged for them to be sent to California to join the five I had already bought that year.

When Mrs McKnight's colt went through the ring, he was gavelled down at $30,000 but I learned later that he went back to Lee Eaton's stable unsold – shades of the year before with An Act. I did go by Lee's consignment and speak with him, but it was in an attempt to convince him that he should advise Mrs McKnight to send him to California so we could sell him in the two-year-old in training sale for her. Lee knew that Mrs McKnight wouldn't want to do that, but he did say she was willing to sell him on the basis of half down and the other half after the sale in California. While this was tempting,

I thought we would have to come up with $15,000 and I had just $10,000 left in my purchasing account. Lee said that he would accept $10,000 down and the balance after the in-training sale. Now I was really tempted but then I discovered that Lee wasn't referring to the $30,000 that was reached in the ring but to Mrs McKnight's minimum price, which was $40,000. This meant that I had to come up with $30,000 after the in-training sale.

I had six months to transform the horse from awful to excellent if we were ever going to succeed with the purchase. I told Lee I needed to sleep on it, but I had the groom lead the colt for me once again. He was an outstanding mover. His stride was impressive and he cruised over the ground like a Rolls-Royce.

I didn't get more than two or three hours' sleep that night, alternately buying the yearling and reselling him very successfully, and then catching hold of myself and deciding I should tell Lee that I couldn't possibly accept the deal.

Alleged as a two-year-old in 1976

I went back out to Keeneland at about six o'clock the next morning and was present as they took the thin, bay colt from his stable to the van that would transport him back to Lee's farm. I examined him closely as he walked the 200 yards to the loading dock. He appeared to have a very good attitude towards people as he was loaded on to the truck. It was this final inspection that made up my mind and I returned to the stable to tell Lee I would take the colt on the terms they wanted. The problem now was how to prepare Pat for the shock of her life. Our investors might also take a dim view of my selection, but it was Pat I was most concerned about.

When the yearlings arrived, she was stunned beyond belief. I was, too, because while the trip from Kentucky to California always sets a yearling back some, this one didn't have any cushion to fall back on. I walked him straight to the horse scale and he registered 649 pounds only. The other yearlings averaged about 950 pounds.

Pat questioned why we had invested in such a challenge as this horse presented. I remember she squared up to me just outside our horse clinic and said, 'That's the last time you're ever going off to a sale by yourself.' She was concerned that this particular purchase was going to derail the outstanding start we had made in selling two-year-olds in training.

It was Pat who came up with the name Alleged. The fact that he was by Hoist the Flag had her playing with the word allegiance, and she eventually applied for and received Alleged. I went to work, first to get him strong enough to accept saddle and rider and then to go through the starting process. Join-up, my secret weapon, was a startling success with Alleged. We began to build up a sense of trust. Alleged took to the environment at Flag Is Up very well and soon reached a weight of about 750 pounds.

Trotting is a very important part of the process I use for the preparation of young horses. It allows for the development of aerobic fitness without any great pressure on the joints. Alleged trotted for approximately ninety days before I asked him to canter, nearly thirty days more than the average yearling. By 1 January, he was around a month behind the rest of the babies but was gaining ground rapidly. He was up to about 950 pounds and was even growing in height, standing nearly 15.3 hands. I was encouraged but still scared to death that I wouldn't get the $40,000 necessary even to recoup the purchase price.

Early in January we had a houseguest by the name of Billy McDonald. Billy was an Irish bloodstock agent who was visiting to observe our consignment as they trained. Billy intended to select one or two of our best yearlings for some clients based in Britain. We'd just received our copy of *Decade of Champions,* illustrated by Richard Stone Reeves. While Billy was reading it, he noticed that Alleged was the offspring of two individuals included in that publication. He flipped to the entries for Hoist the Flag and Princess Pout and told me that I had a rare individual in my consignment.

Billy hadn't seen Alleged and I was extremely nervous as I took him to the stable the following morning. If Billy liked the horse, he might recommend him to potential owners who could afford the high price I needed to achieve. Obviously, the challenge was to present him in such a way that Billy would be pleased with our horse. Alleged was cantering by this time and I must say that his athletic movement overcame many issues about his general condition. Hector Valadez presented Alleged in a very pleasing way.

During lunch that first day, Billy told me he was impressed with the Hoist the Flag colt and wanted to see more of him for the next week or so. Before leaving the farm towards the end of January, Billy seemed to be confident that he could find a customer for our Alleged.

By the time the mid March two-year-old in training sale took place, Alleged weighed well over 1,000 pounds and was very impressive as he negotiated the racetrack at Hollywood Park. Billy McDonald had appeared on the scene about a week before the sale and requested that I refrain from giving Alleged any speed drills because his clients were interested only if there was no pressure put on his immature joints at that early stage. I agreed because I didn't feel he was ready for speed drills either.

However, I was concerned. In an auction sale you need two bidders to elevate the price and buyers might think there was something wrong if we didn't have a speed test to measure Alleged by. It would reduce the buyers' confidence. If that happened, I was likely to get just one bid over my reserve. While I was worried about it, I had given my word and that was it.

Alleged came up to the sales ring looking very well and there seemed to be good interest in him, speed test or no speed test. I had put a $49,500 reserve on him, which would give me nearly $10,000 to cover expenses after the purchase price and could be considered a breakeven sale.

The bidding started at $25,000 and the auctioneer was calling for $50,000 when I saw Billy McDonald raise his hand. I nudged Pat and said, 'We've done it.' Then I heard the auctioneer calling for $75,000 and heard one of the bid spotters yell out, 'Yuuup.'

'Who was that?' Pat asked.

'I don't know. It came from the other side of the ring,' I answered. I couldn't believe what I was seeing as Billy McDonald signalled another bid at $100,000. With that I jumped out of my seat and moved to a position from where I could see who was bidding from the other side. Pat followed me.

The bid spotter was beckoning to a man I knew from Colorado, Hoss Inman. He was in the habit of buying two-year-olds at very reasonable prices for racing at secondary tracks. I almost fell over when I saw Hoss signal a bid at $125,000. Billy came right back with a bid of $150,000, and after what seemed like an eternity, Hoss called out $160,000. The auctioneer asked for $175,000, and Billy responded with another bid. Hoss shook his head, got up and walked out of the pavilion. Pat and I walked over to Billy to congratulate him as he signed the ticket.

I asked Billy who the buyer was and he told me Robert Sangster of England along with two or three other clients. I inquired about who would train him and he told me Vincent O'Brien of Ireland. I had known Vincent for many years and I was happy that Alleged would go to one of the world's leading trainers.

We gave our staff a party that night, and I remember saying a lot of nice things about the job they had done to bring along Alleged so beautifully. Pat and I got to bed about midnight but neither of us slept for more than two or three hours. This time, however, it was a joyful restlessness rather than one of concern.

The phone in our hotel room rang about six-thirty in the morning. It was Billy McDonald. He was in trouble. Robert Sangster had cleared him to pay up to $150,000. He'd been carried away in going to $175,000. Billy asked me if I would take $25,000 off Alleged's price with an agreement that, if he should go to stud, I would be entitled to two breeding rights (shares) in him.

I quickly thought it over and decided the risk was too great. We needed to keep our operation afloat, there were enormous running costs at Flag Is Up

First past the finishing post in the 1978 Arc

and racing was an uncertain business. Alleged may never win enough to earn the right to go to stud and, if he did, he would probably stand in Europe, which would make it very difficult for us to use the breeding rights. I would also have to explain to our investors where the $25,000 had gone. I told Billy that I simply couldn't do it and, with that, he said he thought he could talk Mr Sangster into accepting the full price, which eventually he did.

When Pat did the recap of the consignment that included Alleged, it read as follows: twelve yearlings purchased for $170,000; twelve two-year-olds sold for $503,500. With expenses included, this amounted to a profit of over 350 per cent per annum on a six-month investment. We were ranked first as consignors by gross sales and had the highest-selling individual, Alleged at $175,000, a new record price for a California two-year-old in training.

Alleged was shipped to Vincent O'Brien's Ballydoyle stable and began training immediately. Word soon reached me that Vincent was very pleased with Alleged and he was planning to give him plenty of time to mature. Alleged was given one late start as a two-year-old, and won easily, and was allowed the winter off to prepare for the 1977 racing season, during which he'd be asked to compete against some of the best three-year-olds in the world. Alleged certainly measured up to the task, winning four races before being sent to France for the world's most prestigious horse race, the Prix de l'Arc de Triomphe. This race is open to horses of all ages and so three-year-olds are not often entered for it but, apparently, Alleged impressed Mr O'Brien and his owners so much that they decided to give it a try.

Alleged won, thus becoming the world's leading racehorse for that season. When the news came through, Pat and I were thrilled. This was as good as it gets. When we thought back to the start we'd had with him, it was an awesome feeling.

In 1978 Alleged made three starts and won all three. It was a record-breaking year for him. In the last start of his life, he once again won the Prix de l'Arc de Triomphe and was judged to be the world's champion Thoroughbred racehorse.

Many Americans think that the Kentucky Derby is the most prestigious race in the world, and the Brits feel the same about the English Derby. The fact is that the Prix de l'Arc de Triomphe was, at that time, by far the most important race in the industry.

Alleged's lifetime racing record reads: ten starts, nine wins and one second with earnings of $623,187.

Immediately after the 1978 Arc, it was announced that shares in Alleged were set at $400,000, and within ten days all forty shares were taken. If I had taken them up, my two shares would have been worth $800,000. I kicked myself.

The Alleged syndicate eventually purchased Walmac Farm in Lexington for the purpose of standing him at stud. I went there many times to see him during the course of his breeding career and I often wondered if he remembered his old boss in his time of glory. Did he remember join-up? Did he remember all the good food and exercise we gave him to help him recover? I had had to become almost like a professor in equine nutrition in order to improve his underdeveloped body in six months.

Alleged had an outstanding breeding career. Jockey Club statistics show that, along with his championships in racing at three and four years of age, he was the leading broodmare sire for 1998. He remained on Walmac until his death in 2001 at the age of twenty-seven.

They tell me I should be retired at my age, maybe fishing or lying in a hammock somewhere, but horses such as Alleged still excite these old bones and keep me going. They've given me so much, I can't think of retiring. My excitement and passion for horses won't go away. Each of the horses included in this book has been a powerful contributor to my career but somewhere down inside is the feeling that Alleged shone brighter than most.

NAPUR

In 1978 I bought a colt by Damascus out of a mare called Lodge for $50,000. Pat named him Napur, which happens to be a region near Damascus, and he was a very attractive light chestnut with lots of white on his legs.

I was unable to sell Napur as a two-year-old in training, as I had intended, because of an infection he contracted in those beautiful white legs of his. It's often called 'scratches' or 'dew poisoning'. So I took him home and eventually concluded that he was not likely to withstand the rigours of racing.

My veterinarian, Dr Van Snow, was a fan of show-jumping. We agreed to school Napur to determine whether he might be suited to that discipline.

Napur began to win baby show-jumping contests immediately and, as I recall, we were only about five or six months into the competition phase when Van came to me and said Hap Hanson was interested in showing him. Hap was, and is, one of the leading professional show-jumping riders in the United States and, while this didn't mean we had a champion, it was encouraging.

Van accepted the responsibility of continuing Napur's training and was soon taking him off to some relatively major shows where Hap would ride him in competition. Our team moved up the ladder of competitive show-jumping and after a year they were winning contests ranked at the top of the California circuit.

In his second full year of competition, Napur was competing at Grand Prix level, which placed him among the top two or three hundred horses in the United States. Van suggested sending him to Scandinavia and Europe for the following season. Will Simpson, another top show-jumping rider, was planning

Ridden by Dr Van Snow, Napur shows his perfect form over the Grand Prix wall

a tour of the major horse shows there in 1985 and very much wanted to take Napur, along with three other horses.

We shifted into top gear and Van got Napur into the best condition possible over the six to eight months allocated to preparing for the junket. Napur was very successful on his tour and came back as one of the most promising show-jumping stallions in the world. His ability in the show ring, along with his impeccable pedigree, caused Napur to be well received as a breeding stallion. It was because of those two primary factors that we sold Napur. He eventually went to a show-jumping partnership for a price of $550,000.

Feeling an extremely strong sense of accomplishment, Pat and I had a record to uphold whereby we had sold each of our yearling purchases. While we didn't make the auction ring with Napur, our ultimate sale was more profitable than any of our other yearling purchases for that year. It took a long time to do it, and we had expenses along the way, but it is nevertheless one more piece of evidence that good horsemanship and patience are often partners in success.

Napur helped in a very significant way to broaden the base of my experiences in the horse industry. The show-jumping people would probably see me as a racehorse man; the racehorse people view me as a Western show horse trainer; and the Western show horse people would most likely say that I was a rodeo cowboy. I simply don't care how human beings view me. My only concern is how horses see me.

MUSTANG MARE

Throughout my career I had been secretly using join-up as a technique for communicating with horses and developing a relationship with them based on trust. The round pen at my first training establishment, in San Luis Obispo, was across a creek, well away from where anyone could see it. At Flag Is Up, which was crowded with horses and staff, the covered round pens had been built with solid tongue and groove sides. There wasn't a crack for anyone to see in. Any riders or horsemen around the place would have thought I was exercising a horse in circles. It had become a habit never to mention it.

By the mid eighties, I had started literally thousands of babies using join-up. After forty years' experience, it had become predictable and extremely effective. Domestic horses would normally join with me and follow me around in ten minutes or so, with their noses at my shoulder. Within fifteen minutes, they would be willing to stand for the first saddle of their lives. A rider was usually on their backs in an average of thirty minutes.

Like snowflakes, every horse is different, but when you come to know the true nature of these flight animals, the similarities far outweigh the differences. Barlet, for instance, was a very aggressive horse and, while I could do join-up with him, I had to be careful, but the procedure changed him dramatically. For Johnny Tivio, on the other hand, perhaps the most important horse in my life and therefore left until the end of this book, join-up was vastly different. It was as though someone said to him come and join the party and instantly things began to take shape. With Bahroona, Sharivari, An Act and

Alleged, join-up served to foster a feeling that every other trainer was working with handcuffs on and his legs chained together. Join-up seemed to give me that kind of advantage. I didn't feel I was keeping the knowledge of join-up from the rest of the world – I didn't think they wanted to know about it.

One day, I was starting a baby in the round pen while, just twenty yards away, some men were working on a tree that had been damaged by a storm. Thoroughbred trainer Farrell Jones came to have a look at the tree and was lifted up in a hydraulic hoist just outside the round pen. As chance would have it, the broken branch was at precisely the right height to allow him to see over the side wall, underneath the roof and directly into the round pen. I wasn't aware of it, but he could see everything that was going on.

Farrell was puzzled – and certainly surprised. When I came out he asked me what was going on. He wondered if he could believe his eyes. I found myself telling him the basics – not without some sense of dread. His interest increased and he wouldn't leave me alone about it.

I was used to nothing but rejection and disbelief when it came to what I could do with join-up. The instinct to keep it under wraps had never left me, yet the opposite instinct – to tell everyone – was also very strong. I was convinced I had something that would transform the relationship between mankind and the horse forever.

Farrell wanted to tell other people about what he'd seen.

'Hell no,' I said. 'That would get me into no end of trouble.'

He asked me to give a demonstration for invited guests but I refused. He made the point that I had something truly important to show to the horse world and I agreed but it seemed like the rest of the world didn't want to know. He said it was my duty to give a demonstration and that was true. I did feel a sense of duty about it. In my heart I knew it was something I should share but it was a risk I wasn't willing to take. The time was always wrong to bring it out into the open. I was scared of jeopardizing a successful career in Thoroughbred racing. I didn't want to be regarded as a kook. I was quite open with him. It wouldn't be good for business. He thought the opposite and that nothing but good could come of it.

'You'd think so,' I replied, 'but it hasn't been the case so far.'

In the end he persuaded me. He organized a demonstration to which he invited notable horse people of the area, as well as journalists. Articles were written in various horse publications. A lot of people talked about it. Others came to watch. I built a ramp up to a viewing gallery around the outside of the round pen, so now people could see in. Interest in what I was doing began to grow.

However, business at Flag Is Up Farms slumped; it fell by a quarter immediately afterwards. I didn't have the heart to tell Farrell. I watched the number of horses in training start to go down. It was happening, just as I thought it would. Apparently, many trainers felt insecure because they didn't understand my concepts. It seems that what they didn't understand frightened them and they backed away. Change was in the wind and I could either fight against it or go with it. As usual, it was the horses that carried me.

Around this time, I experienced an episode of join-up that must rank as one of the most extraordinary pieces of communication between species of all time.

I received a call one day from a lady who had just adopted a mustang mare from the Bureau of Land Management (BLM). The mare had a foal at her side, approximately five months old. The new owner had heard about the work I was doing – perhaps she'd read one of the articles, I don't exactly remember. In any case, she wanted me to start her mare. She intended to ride her and later pass her on to her children. I advised her to wean the foal first and when they were well separated, I would put the mare through the starting process.

Ten days or so later, the lady arrived with her mare. She backed her trailer up to my round pen and released one of the wildest animals you could imagine. She told me the only interaction the mustang had had with humans was when they brought feed and water to her. As I viewed the mare, she seemed a daunting challenge.

Eventually, I entered the pen and began my work. I decided to take my time and give her all the space she needed. There was no hurry. The mare gave me all the signs of communication and was soon taking steps towards me. After about forty-five minutes I was touching her and by the two-hour mark I had a halter on her and was leading her around. I could pick up her front feet but when I tried to pick up the back ones she kicked with fury. Soon I could rub her body on both sides and she would volunteer to stay with me, not taking the slack out of the lead rope.

In just over two hours, I indicated to my rider, Sean McCarthy, that he should bring in a saddle, bridle, saddle pad and another long line. While he was doing this, the mare was hovering very close to me at the south side of the pen. Sean left through a gate on the north side, closing it to leave me alone with the mare, an eight-foot high solid wall all around us.

I started to walk towards the equipment that had been placed in the centre of the circle and the mare began to follow, but as we took two or three steps from the south wall, she passed me like a rocket. Running as fast as she could, she crashed into the saddle on the ground and started ripping it to shreds with her teeth. It was as if Sean had brought a lion into the middle of the pen and she had to kill it or die herself.

I froze in my tracks, still near the south wall. The air was filled with bits and pieces as they flew off the saddle. It was terrifying and I was pretty sure I was next on the menu. I started moving to my right, staying as close to the wall as I could. I was aiming to get around to the door on the north side, and out of the pen. I remember I moved as smoothly and rapidly as possible. I had recently had extensive back surgery and jumping the eight-foot wall was out of the question.

I'd made it about halfway to the door when the mare broke away from the saddle and ran straight at me. I was still about forty feet from the gate – too far to run. I fell to my knees next to the wall and balled up on the ground in a foetal position, covering my head with my hands. Sean was on the observation stand near the gate and I remember he jumped down into the pen just as the mare reached me. I was certain she would attack me, just as she had done the saddle but she slid to a stop, virtually covering me with dirt. She blasted into a position just over me, and I got ready for something that wasn't going to be pretty. Her feet ripped at the ground, throwing clods of dirt on me. The noise was deafening and my mind prepared for bolts of pain to start shooting through me, anticipating the onslaught of her teeth and hooves. The noise subsided and the pain failed to occur. I don't remember even being touched by one of those flying feet.

Balled up on the ground, I could see the mare's head out of the corner of my eye. Her nose was near the wall in front of me and her hind feet were doing a dance near my toes. She was actually right over the top of me when I saw her look directly at the saddle and pin her ears flat back on her neck.

Within a second or two, she looked back towards me and her ears came forward. She wasn't attacking me at all. She was protecting me from that evil saddle. She'd recently been weaned from her foal and, with join-up, she'd adopted me instead.

I called out to Sean, 'Wait, don't come closer yet.' The mare, it seemed, had not even noticed Sean.

It must have been five seconds or so, but it felt like an hour, when the mare suddenly left me like a bolt of lightning. She made what turned out to be one last run at that saddle, grabbed a piece of it, gave it a toss and then, before I could even move from my position, returned just as fast as she left me. Standing guard over me once again, the mare resumed the pattern of looking at the saddle with her ears flat back, then looking at me with her ears forward, concerned for my safety.

Within a few seconds, I began to feel a slight tapping on my jeans near my ankles and felt the sensation of warm fluid where my pants legs had ridden up, exposing some skin. I looked back when it seemed safe and realized she still had milk in her udder, which was now dripping on to my legs. Join-up had aroused her maternal instinct.

Sean began to pick up the bits and pieces of the saddle, and soon he returned with a second one. We didn't put this one down in the middle of the pen and I managed to saddle her with virtually no trouble. After another twenty minutes or so, Sean was riding on her back. Our nerves were frayed but the session ended on a calm note.

I recall a phrase that kept coming into my mind – 'the power of join-up'. This mare had shown me a new dimension in the effect of join-up. It wasn't just that she trusted me – she was motivated to protect me.

The mustang mare became a gentle mount for the lady and her children. I have been told they won many trophies at mustang horse shows, and for the balance of her days she was a trustworthy part of her adopted family.

Interestingly, ancient cave drawings have been discovered over a wide geographical area, wherever horses have existed for thousands of years. The drawings bear a remarkable resemblance to one another, and depict a human child on hands and knees nursing from a tiny mare appropriate in size to the early developing horses. I don't know whether that situation ever occurred or not but I am far more prepared to accept the possibility now than I ever was before my experience with this mustang mare. When I began to work with her, I knew she was wild. Her level of trust for a human being was non-existent. At the time the milk dripped on my legs, she not only trusted me, she had actively included me, and I was her responsibility, her child.

If ever we needed evidence of the theory that horses can become partners with human beings, that was it. Whether we compete on horses or keep them for pleasure, we should be ever mindful of this mustang mare and her message to us that horses can be true friends and even protectors.

There are many lessons here but I believe the most important one is that the proper execution of non-violent join-up will engender trust. The actions of predators during the mare's formative years were probably responsible, at least in part, for her response. I don't think a domestic mare would have reacted in this manner. Predators educate their prey to protect their young at all costs. I had underestimated the power of join-up.

THE QUEEN MOTHER'S FILLY

After the demonstration of join-up at Flag Is Up Farms, Her Majesty the Queen, a keen horsewoman and racehorse owner, happened to read about it in *The Blood Horse* and *Florida Horse* magazines. She instructed her equerry (horse manager) Sir John Miller to get in touch with me because she was intrigued and wanted to investigate my claims. Sir John Miller telephoned a friend of his in California, a certain John Bowles, and asked him if he'd ever heard of this character Monty Roberts?

'I've known him for fifteen years and he lives five miles down the road,' John Bowles replied, and offered to call me. When he rang and said the Queen of England wanted to meet me, I thought he was joking.

Not long afterwards, Sir John Miller came to see for himself what I could do and we arranged a demonstration especially for him. He was very excited by it and told me the Queen would certainly be inviting me to come to England and give just such a demonstration to an invited audience. Sure enough, in February 1989, Pat and I received an invitation to Windsor Castle for April of that year. Her Majesty's staff would arrange for horses and a round pen while we would provide a rider, Sean McCarthy.

The circumstances surrounding this and subsequent visits to Windsor Castle have been told in my first book, as well as in many horse magazines, but one horse in particular stands out. She was responsible for ushering in a whole new era of my life – a brown filly owned by Queen Elizabeth, the Queen Mother.

I arrived at London Heathrow on a Saturday morning to be met by Sir John Miller. Pat, our son Marty and Sean were coming the next day. Sir John took me directly to Windsor and soon we were walking through the fields just below the Castle, overlooking Windsor Great Park. The Queen's riding horses were grazing, separately, in small, green fields of about two acres. A larger field, near the main gates of the park, held fifteen head of assorted breeds and colours. These were the horses that had been brought in for me to work with. Sir John told me they would eventually be carriage horses, ceremonial horses and possibly even officers' mounts.

As we wandered further from the stables, we came to a small field where a filly was playing on her own and calling out to the others. Sir John told me she was a Thoroughbred from a sire and dam that were important in the world of steeplechasing. 'She belongs to the Queen Mother,' he said. The plan was to start with this filly at nine o'clock on Monday morning, and he hoped that the Queen Mother would be able to attend.

We discussed the schedule as we walked back to the stables. I said I would like all the horses to be led up to and through the riding school and round pen the following day, Sunday, so they would at least be slightly acquainted with the trip and the environment. Sir John agreed this would be done. He told me the Queen was having lunch with Mikhail and Raisa Gorbachev but that Her Majesty would be available to welcome me and discuss the upcoming week.

We were staying at Shotover House, near Windsor, as guests of Sir John, and he had me back on the Windsor grounds at eight the next morning. With the help of some grooms, I set about bringing the horses to the riding hall for a walk through the round pen.

The Queen was out riding and I was introduced to her on her return. The experience was overwhelming but she immediately put me at ease. She asked me about the wire mesh round pen and suggested it looked a little like a lion's cage. In fact, I'd never worked horses in a pen of this type, but it certainly allowed an audience to see what you were doing. I felt I was in the presence of a good student of horsemanship, who was genuinely interested in what I did. While I never lost sight of the fact that this was the Queen of England, my visit centred on horses and my concepts of working with them and we were able to converse freely. More than twenty subsequent visits have proved my first impression was valid.

Sir John told me that the Queen would come to the first demonstration, with her mother's brown filly, but that her appointments would make it impossible for her to attend for the rest of the week. Arrangements had been made to videotape each day's demonstrations so that she could watch them in the evening.

Monday morning was glorious. Blue skies with big, white clouds ushered in a day that Marty, Sean, Pat and I would remember for the rest of our lives. By nine o'clock, around two hundred guests, including many dignitaries, had gathered. The Queen, Prince Philip and the Queen Mother invited Pat and Marty to watch with them from a private viewing room. Having been introduced to the Queen Mother, I stood with Sir John Miller by a large door at the end of the riding hall. Everything was ready for me to enter the round pen with the Queen Mother's filly.

My heart was racing a mile a minute and my adrenaline level was off the chart. It suddenly struck me that my work could not go well while I was in that state. I constantly tell my students to keep pulse rates low and adrenaline down because horses will tune in to them. They will have high pulse rates if we do. How in the world could I live by my own advice under these circumstances? Through a fog I remember Sir John introducing me to the audience, then leaving the round pen and clicking the latch behind him.

As soon as I released the filly and she began to move away, a state of calm came over me. I think my muscles and some portion of my subconscious brain took over at that point and automatically performed the procedures that four decades of experience had taught me. Obviously, I had never worked under these circumstances before. Somehow, the presence of the Queen Mother was more daunting to me than that of the Queen, Prince Philip or the guests and dignitaries. I suppose, as a professional horseman, more than anything else you tend to seek the approval of the owner of the animal you are working with, no matter who else is present.

Through the grace of God and a filly that seemed to know how important it was, I managed to get through a good join-up and she accepted her first saddle, bridle and rider. Sean appeared to be quite calm and did a great job despite the pressurized environment. The filly quietly followed me around the pen after the saddle was removed and clearly demonstrated her acceptance of my non-violent technique of starting horses.

I became very conscious of the door through which I expected to see the royal family emerge, as well as Marty and Pat. The Queen was the first to appear and, with right hand extended, she approached me saying that my demonstration was extraordinary. Her Majesty's greeting was warm and it was clear that she had been affected by what the last half-hour had shown. Although I was totally uninformed regarding protocol with the royal family, I was now relaxed so I just let events progress as they felt comfortable to me.

Prince Philip was the next to appear. He walked briskly towards me, grabbed my hand with the strength of an athlete and slapped me on the shoulder with a firm gesture of approval. He asked me if I would work with some of his driving ponies during the week and, of course, I agreed.

For a moment, everything seemed to stand still as I awaited my owner. The Queen Mother emerged and walked slowly towards me, with Pat following. The emotion she showed surprised me. I noticed a tear as she reached out her two hands to greet me. I took both of them and she said it was one of the most beautiful displays she'd ever witnessed. Instinctively, I put my right arm around the Queen Mother's shoulders. The security people stiffened and stepped forwards and I was suddenly aware of what I was doing. The etiquette is never to touch a member of the royal family. I quickly removed my arm and moved back but Her Majesty continued to squeeze my left hand and, clearly filled with emotion, stepped closer to me. She told me to continue my work to bring about a better relationship between humans and horses for as long as I could.

At the gate of the round pen, the Queen Mother shook Sean's hand and thanked him for his part in the proceedings, while rubbing her filly's nose. The Queen, Sir John, Pat and I escorted her to her car. As we returned to the riding hall, I thanked the Queen for the time she had given me that morning and hoped she would be able to watch the videos of the rest of the week's work. Her Majesty replied that, with her schedule so packed with appointments, the videos were the only way she would be able to see it. She went on to say that, at the conclusion of the week, Sir John Miller would assist with arranging a tour to include twenty-one stops in England. It was quite clear that the Queen of England had enjoyed my demonstration and wanted English horsemen and women to see it.

Back inside the riding hall, we took some pictures with the Queen Mother's filly and mingled with the guests before going off to lunch at the Savile

A work day for the Queen, the Queen Mother's Filly and me in the riding hall, Windsor Castle, 1989

Gardens in Windsor Park. As I posed for pictures with the filly, I began to recognize her importance to me. The Queen had just asked me to do a tour. This was a royal request and, of course, I answered affirmatively. It was only later that I learned how rare this type of endorsement is. She also gave her approval for an article and photograph to appear in *Horse & Hound* magazine. Michael Clayton, then the editor of the magazine, was one of the invited guests, and he wrote the article himself.

Pat and I didn't know at the time, but adjustments were being made to the Queen's schedule so that she and Prince Philip could come to watch the afternoon's proceedings, and she was present for almost eight hours on each of the five days I worked at Windsor Castle. I managed to start more than twenty horses during that time and the Queen told me I must write a book to tell the world about my concepts. The Queen Mother's filly was ridden each day and on Friday her royal owner returned to see this beautiful young Thoroughbred carrying her rider, Sean, calmly through the Windsor Gardens, accompanied by the Queen's stud groom of that time, Roger Oliver, riding a trained horse.

Not long afterwards we visited each of the cities on Sir John's schedule and completed the Queen's tour by 18 May, returning to Windsor Castle with a report of events. I wrote the book, as the Queen suggested, and more than any other one element *The Man Who Listens to Horses* altered the course of my career and my life.

My relationship with the Queen has remained strong over the years and I was invited to attend her fifty-year jubilee in May 2002 on the very grounds where it all began, back in 1989.

Sure, there are important horses in my life, world champions and high performers of every sort, but this dark brown filly was a fulcrum. My life changed direction and I found myself becoming a writer and educator, touring the world giving demonstrations of join-up. I often think back to the scepticism and disbelief I suffered as a child and the shadow it cast over the next forty years. That has been lifted now. Join-up has been met with a level of acceptance I could never have believed possible, and the Queen Mother's filly started it.

The Queen Mother's Filly in Windsor gardens, Sean McCarthy up, accompanied by Her Majesty, the Queen Mother, our son Marty, myself, and Pat

STANLEY

The California Thoroughbred Breeders Association had discontinued their agreement with Hollywood Park. The major California two-year-old sales venue would from now on be the Pomona Race Track about fifteen miles east of Santa Anita. Previews would be conducted at this half-mile track with virtually every entry being asked to gallop one-eighth of a mile (220 metres). This became a different game entirely, and Pat and I were not prepared to push babies to perform one furlong in ten seconds. For nineteen years our consignments led the world in producing two-year-olds prepared for racing but now our lives were obliged to take a different path.

With join-up finally coming out into the open, I developed a missionary zeal about educating as many people as possible. At the same time, more and more people were requesting that I use my experience to deal with remedial cases. So I moved into a phase of my life where I would answer the call of many owners and trainers around the world to deal with specific problems that beset their horses. I became a travelling horse psychologist.

Horse & Hound magazine asked me to conduct some all-day teaching clinics at Stoneleigh and Towerlands and, once again, I went to see the Queen. I came away from this meeting clearly aware of her desire for me to conduct a demonstration tour in Ireland. During that trip I met a horse that carved out a notch in my memory that will never fade. His name was Stanley. He was a three-year-old Irish draught stallion and for various reasons he'd become very aggressive and extremely dangerous.

A member of the Queen's staff asked me to telephone Hugh McCusker of Lurgan, near Belfast, who would organize the tour. I was surprised when I got him on the phone because he was sceptical and quite reticent. He told me that a lady had talked to him by telephone but she'd said some things that seemed quite bizarre – something about communicating with horses and causing them to accept their first saddle, bridle and rider in about thirty minutes. Hugh McCusker went on to say that he wasn't interested in getting involved with 'hocus pocus' stuff. He told me that if I wanted him to represent me on a tour of Ireland, I would have to go to Belfast and convince him there was good reason to consider this effort.

I was shocked by the conversation but I had faced this kind of scepticism for most of my life and knew I could answer it, so I boarded a plane for Belfast. A driver picked me up at the airport and took me to the McCusker home in Lurgan. I was introduced to Hugh, who was a big man with sandy hair, bushy eyebrows and a handshake that would crush steel bars. He sat me down in his living room and put me through a strong session of questions about what I might show the people, expressing grave doubt that it would work.

Hugh said that Irish horses were much tougher than those in England, and my claims seemed outrageous to him. He announced that he had set up a little test involving a horse that had been recently rescued from an abusive environment. He said I could back out of this if I wanted to because the horse was no pushover. I agreed to his test and we drove together for about twenty miles to an indoor riding arena.

About fifteen to twenty people were waiting when we arrived, and they brought in a thin gelding about five years old with a large open gash between his eyes and down the bridge of his nose. When I asked what had happened to the horse, his handler told me that he'd had an argument with a blackthorn limb. Hugh explained that in Ireland it meant a kind of a club that, apparently, was used to hit the horse. The poor creature was frightened and needed a friend. I had a rider on his back in less than thirty minutes, and all I can remember Hugh saying was, 'Full marks. I give you full marks. You're going on tour.' Hugh had a background of producing show hunters and was the master of the hounds in his part of the world. He had great confidence and a flamboyant personality and he had put me through a test, as only a good Irishman could.

Around twelve cities were included on Hugh's schedule, spread out from top to bottom of the Emerald Isle. One of the last stops was located just outside Dublin and called, ominously, Kill. This is home to one of Ireland's most famous horsewomen, Iris Kellet. She'd recently sold her original training centre to the president of the Irish Draught Association, Fenton Flannely, and apparently he wanted my event to serve as an open house to the community.

The plan was to start two of Fenton Flannely's Irish draught fillies that had never been ridden. He said they'd have a coffee and cake session afterwards, and I was to meet people and answer questions about what they had just seen. I agreed to this slightly different format and we arrived at the facility at approximately two o'clock in the afternoon.

The event began at seven-thirty in the evening and, with an introduction and a bit of time between the two fillies, I had both of them comfortably ridden just after nine. During the coffee and cake session, Hugh mentioned that Fenton Flannely was very impressed with what he had seen and would be very happy if I would work with one more horse for him after the refreshments. I remember asking Hugh if he thought the 500 people in attendance would want to stay for a horse to be done after ten o'clock. He thought a lot of them would go home but this last horse was mostly for Fenton Flannely.

As soon as the word got back to him that I had agreed to do his third horse, he made an announcement over the public address system. 'Monty has agreed to work with my three-year-old stallion, Stanley. As you all know, he's never been saddled or ridden and if any of you would like to stay after the coffee, you're welcome.' People started to whisper and I sensed a feeling of excitement running through the audience. I asked Hugh what was going on but I don't recall getting a satisfactory answer.

When the audience was once again seated, it was apparent to me that more people were there than before the coffee break. I didn't understand how we could have an audience grow after ten at night. Hugh said he supposed this horse was of interest to them, and maybe they had called family and friends encouraging them to come to see me work with Stanley.

'Yeah,' I said. 'That's what I'm thinking, too, but I'm not so sure it's because they think he's wonderful. I have a feeling they sense some real drama here.'

From a very early age, I've attended jackpot ropings and match races and been exposed to every trick that horsemen play on one another. I didn't need a newspaper to tell me what was going on. The community knew this horse and it was probably not because he was a lovable teddy bear. I sat back quietly and began to observe the proceedings. What had I let myself in for?

When my late-night subject arrived, he had two strong Irish lads leading him, one on each side. They were followed by one of Fenton Flannely's trainers, Ronnie McComb. The lads had long leads, each one with a chain over the horse's nose. I noticed it was a bit tricky to get him through a four-foot gate and into my round pen. It was easy to see that he was aggressive, and the expression on the faces of the boys told a large part of the story. They knew they were bringing Hannibal Lecter himself into the building, and he wasn't wearing a muzzle.

The boys carefully turned him loose and it was crystal clear that this large chestnut had an appetite for human flesh. With the lads outside the pen and the gate closed, there was silence, which was odd considering there were now nearly 600 people in a small area. Fenton Flannely took the microphone and told the audience I was going to work with Stanley. He said that this horse had been a champion when shown in hand, but that not much had been done with him for the past year.

As Fenton Flannely spoke, I watched this beautiful Irish draught horse circling the pen, intermittently walking, trotting and cantering. I could easily see why he was a champion in hand. He had a strong set of legs and a body that was balanced and symmetrical. His muscular neck and beautiful head indicated that he was probably more intelligent than his handlers wanted him to be. He moved with a grace and strength that was almost frightening to watch.

With my lapel mike open, I asked why nothing had been done with him for a year, and the answer was that he had become a bit of a handful the last time he was shown. They had decided to leave him alone for a while in the hopes that he would become a little friendlier towards people. I inquired whether they thought it had worked but I don't think I got a response to that question.

With Stanley standing at the far side of the pen, I went in through the small gate and stepped a couple of paces towards him. He flew into a rage, pinned his ears flat on his neck and ran straight at me, mouth open and teeth exposed in a great imitation of a Bengal tiger. You could hear a collective gasp as I made it out of the gate and closed it just in time. Stanley came to a stop just at the other side of the fence and began to pace like a zoo-bound lion. 'Holey, moley!' I called out to my audience. Stanley walked back and forth inside the pen, moving his ears and snapping at the mesh wire.

I sat down on a chair next to my equipment bag. I will never forget the next few minutes because, whether these Irishmen knew it or not, I was very concerned for my safety. There's no doubt in my mind that if my health insurance agent had been there that night, he would have cancelled my policy on the spot. I relaxed for a minute, trying to think of a course of action. It went through my head that there would be articles in the paper the next day telling of either great failure or great success, or possibly there would just be a long list of injuries to a fifty-four-year-old Californian who thought he could handle a difficult Irish horse. Deciding to buy another minute or so, I had a conversation with the audience.

'What the heck are you trying to do to me?' I inquired. 'I'm an old man. I retired from the rodeo arena twenty-five years ago. Five of my vertebrae are welded together. I'll be killed if I go in with this equine carnivore. Surely, the nice people of Ireland wouldn't set me up. Would they? On this trip I've met a lot of sceptical people who feel that some of my work is less than believable.'

While I spoke, I scanned the audience and it was easy to see that many people there were young, healthy and, by the look of them, probably competent horsemen. I went on to play a game with them.

'So I would like to have a volunteer,' I said. 'There are undoubtedly some very good horsemen here, who are younger and stronger than I am. I'll stand outside the pen and give advice if a volunteer will go in there and deal with this horse.'

You could have heard a pin drop. The backside of every pair of trousers in the building was welded to the seat.

'Ahh,' I said, 'doesn't look like I'm going to get any volunteers. Guess I'll just have to do this one myself.'

Join-up in its true form was out of the question. I had to get control of the situation before I could persuade this horse to trust me. I dug to the bottom of my bag and came out with a nylon lariat rope, the kind I had won a National Team Roping Championship with so many years before. I opened the gate once more and asked my rider to close it behind me. The instant I was in the pen I began to swing the rope around my head. Horses are inherently frightened of anything unfamiliar. Generally, flight animals will flee from something they don't understand. I hoped to create an image that Stanley had never seen before, and cause him to stay away from me for a few seconds.

I walked towards the middle and watched Stanley closely as he tried to size me up. He seemed unable to come to grips with this strange sight and began to circle me, walking with his neck arched high. At the appropriate moment, I cast a loop that found its way around his neck just behind his jaws. As I drew it down, Stanley went into a bucking rage. He squalled and groaned,

Stanley as a mature stallion

sounding more like a grizzly bear than a horse. Now he had a new concern. I was not the problem, the rope was. I gave him a little tug now and then, and he would go into a renewed orbit, expressing all the rage he had locked up inside him.

If there were 600 people in that building, I had 1,200 eyes directly on Stanley and me, and not even one was blinking. After about thirty or forty seconds, Stanley came to a stop. I moved in immediately, making the rope into the kind of halter I had used for many years to control difficult horses. The instant my rope was in place, Stanley began to cooperate. He went quiet and I didn't waste any time getting a saddle and bridle on him.

I rigged Stanley up on the long lines, even quicker than I would normally do with a non-aggressive horse, and once on the lines I put him to work. I long-lined him for almost ten minutes instead of the normal two or three. In order to prepare him for my rider, I knew I had to do a fair bit of work. Excess energy with this big guy could prove to be lethal. At the appropriate moment, I brought in my rider, who happened to be an Irish racing exercise rider, Dermot O'Sullivan. He was a game lad to get on this incredible creature with the power of two normal horses. As I put him up, he said he thought the safest place to be in that round pen was actually on top of Stanley.

With a rider in the saddle, Stanley went to work in an orderly fashion. Once more, I gave him far more work to do than I would a normal horse. He took it well and we finished the evening with our audience amazed and full of questions. They surrounded me as soon as I left the round pen and it was probably after midnight before Hugh and Fenton Flannely could pull me away. We went to Fenton's house for a drink and more conversation than I ever wanted to go through.

Fenton confessed that Stanley had got vicious at the Dublin Horse Show a year before. He'd injured two people and been put in a dark box stall. Nobody had handled him since then, until that night. Ronnie McComb spoke up and said what they had just witnessed was unbelievable. This was one of the most vicious horses anyone had ever known. Ronnie went on to tell me that Stanley had set out to kill somebody on several different occasions in the past twelve months. I wanted to ask what the heck they were thinking about, putting me in there without telling me these things, but somehow I knew they wouldn't have an acceptable answer anyway, so I didn't bother asking.

Five years later, in 1995, I returned to Fenton Flannely's place. After the intermission, when I returned from a question and answer session, I was surprised to see some fences in the arena but really didn't think much of it until Hugh McCusker and the rest of the team unveiled their surprise. Over the public address system a voice said, 'Monty, this is Stanley. He is now Ireland's finest show-jumping Irish draught horse.'

Stanley came into the ring groomed as if he was at a championship show, his mane braided. His lady rider took him in a large circle to give the audience a chance to appreciate how beautiful he was. She guided Stanley towards the first fence. Over he popped like a Thompson's gazelle and proceeded to jump each of the fences they had set for him. He stopped in the middle of the arena and his rider bowed slightly to the crowd. Then the announcer read what they said was a message from Stanley:

'Thank you for saving my life. They were about to send me on a one-way trip when I met you, Mr Roberts, and I couldn't have blamed them for doing it. I was a very bad boy and I hated people, but you took the time to show me that it was OK to trust again. I am a champion now and I have you to thank for that.'

I just stood there with tears running down my cheeks.

PRINCE OF DARKNESS

One day the phone rang and it was Sir Mark Prescott, a trainer in Newmarket. He said he had a horse called Prince of Darkness, owned by a partnership including both English and Americans. This was a horse with talent, but he had an absolute phobia about the starting gate (starting stalls).

By now, I leased a facility in England – Bernice Cuthbert's Aston Park Stud. I wanted a base so remedial horses could be sent to me and I wouldn't have to travel as much, which would enable me to spend more time actually working on their problems. Sir Mark made arrangements to send Prince of Darkness to Aston Park Stud.

By any standards Prince of Darkness was huge – he stood about 17.0 hands high and had a body with far more muscling than you normally see on a potential racehorse. He had a reputation for being a tough guy and there were many stories about him coming from the farm in Ireland where he was raised.

'He killed a steer when he was a yearling,' his groom warned me. She told me that the Prince had become extremely dangerous when anywhere near the starting gate.

I worked with him for about four days and while he seemed a bit disturbed by the stalls, I had him entering, standing quietly and leaving them before sending him back to Newmarket.

A week or so later I was back in California when a call came through and I immediately recognized Sir Mark's voice.

'Do you stand behind your work?' he asked.

'Sure I do. What's the problem?' I replied.

'This horse is not fixed and I need you here immediately because I have some impatient owners who want results as soon as possible.'

I was in Newmarket within a few days. Sir Mark, the groom and the exercise rider sat down with me and we reviewed every experience they could tell me about.

It seems that this enormous two-year-old was fine with the gates for the first couple of training sessions. The third time the Prince was schooled, he hesitated before fully entering the gate. Somebody tapped him on a thigh and he kicked back, hitting the rear portion of the apparatus. From that point on, Prince of Darkness hated the sight of the heap of metal and became a danger both to his handlers and himself.

I stayed with Sir Mark at Heath House and it took the next three days to bring Prince of Darkness to the same point I had achieved on my earlier trip. This time, however, the Prince was never relaxed in the stall and was inclined to kick frequently and would even attempt to bite me as I worked near his head. Something was very wrong with this environment compared to the one at Aston Park. I explained my dilemma to Sir Mark and told him I suspected that the foot rails along the sides of the official gates were much larger than in the stalls I had originally used.

If simple claustrophobia was the culprit, it might be helpful to order up a horse-box with adjustable partitions so I could squeeze Prince of Darkness into a very narrow space, which would allow me to test him while he was being driven, to see what his response might be. Sir Mark agreed and we scheduled the horse-box for the following morning.

Sir Mark and I had dinner and a couple glasses of wine while I suppose I droned on about being frustrated to the tenth power. I told him that I was one sore, beat-up fifty-five-year-old cowboy. Prince had bitten me several times, bashed me into the walls of the starting gate and had run square over the top of me on two different occasions.

'I'm at my wits' end,' I said. I didn't understand how I could get him fixed and then have him go back to square one, time after time. It crossed my mind several times to suggest that I return the fees and walk away.

We got to bed about ten o'clock, one hour late for Sir Mark, and I made every attempt to get a good night's rest but sleep refused to come. My mind kept doing playbacks of my work. I'd start to doze off and then one silly idea or another would hit me and I would be wide awake trying to make sense of plan after plan as they passed through my wholly incompetent brain.

At around two in the morning I found myself pacing up and down the hall outside my upstairs bedroom. Soft footsteps sounded and a door opened to reveal Sir Mark looking at me quizzically. Wrapped in a bathrobe, he stood in his doorway, silently questioning why I was walking up and down, disturbing his sleep, too. We blinked at each other for a few seconds before I spoke.

'I'm sorry if I disturbed you, but I can't sleep. I can't seem to get my brain to stop working.'

Appearing to sympathize with me, Sir Mark came and stood near the window, with his face cast in moonlight. Suddenly his expression sharpened.

'Well, I'll be,' he muttered softly. 'Come and see this.'

I went and stood next to him and from the window we could see over the sloping roof of the house to the stable yard below. In the moonlight we could clearly make out Prince of Darkness, his head appearing first at the window of his stall and then at the door as he walked back and forth. The Prince was just as awake as we were.

Sir Mark sighed. 'That's three of us trying to work out what the heck is wrong.'

Sir Mark told me that the name Prince of Darkness came about because the horse had killed that steer in his paddock in Ireland and played with it like a cat with a mouse. He said the starting gates were just not built for a horse his size. He reminded me that when the Prince was in the starting stall, his nose touched the front gate while his hindquarters were crowded by the rear one. He also mentioned that he could see the foot rails pressing into his sides even when the Prince was standing quietly.

'Now I'm going to leave the two of you to execute your gentle battle of wills,' he said. Sir Mark needed to be in the stable by five and he had to get some sleep. 'You two work on your problems as quietly as you can, and if you have to give up, I'll notify the owners. While I don't know if they'll understand, I certainly will.'

The horse-box arrived about seven o'clock the following morning. The results of the tests proved I could squeeze him as tightly as I wanted while the driver negotiated sharp turns all around Newmarket without a negative response from the Prince. So he didn't mind being hemmed in and claustrophobia was not the answer. We returned to Heath House and I reported the results to Sir Mark. I was excited to at least discover something about our problem.

Warren Hill was only about half a mile away, Henry Cecil's yard, where a training stall I had designed was in place. Henry agreed that I could work Prince of Darkness there and off we went. My training stall was built so that the foot rails could be removed and I began to work with the Prince with no rails at all. Lo and behold, he was the perfect student. I replaced the rails and put the Prince back in the stall. I stood in front of him and moved him slightly forward and back, as I often do to test a horse's acceptance of the stall, and he exploded, knocking me down again and running right over the top of me. I had a thirty-foot line on him so he didn't get loose, but I was nearly unconscious as I staggered up with the Prince at the end of the line. I remember the groom was there along with a friend of Sir Mark's, Geraldine Rees, who happened to be the first woman ever to complete the Grand National. They both ran over and Geraldine pointed out that I was bleeding from a laceration by my left ear.

'It's the rails,' I exclaimed. 'We need to remove the rails and everything will be OK.'

Geraldine gave me a ride down the hill to Heath House where I washed my ear and stuck a plaster on it while Sir Mark phoned a racing steward he knew. Apparently, it was not allowed to change the starting gate in any way. We would just have to figure out how to live with the rails.

As I explained to Sir Mark, I believed that the Prince felt as though the rails were biting him. When he kicked out, the rails caused more pain, reinforcing that idea. This intuitive reaction goes back to a time when wolves or packs of dogs attacked his ancestors.

Geraldine drove me back to Warren Hill and I took up where I left off. The training stall allowed me to school with no rails, very small rails and medium rails, as well as with regulation-size rails. Prince of Darkness could handle the tiny ones and that was it. With anything larger, he would return to being a demon. I was in a sorry state of discouragement when I began to mutter to Geraldine about a thought that was passing through my head.

'You know those leather pads that protect the picador's horse in Spanish bull fights?' I asked. Geraldine knew exactly what I was referring to. I went on to say that if I could cover the Prince's hips with a very heavy leather blanket, it might be possible to eliminate the feel of the rails. The trip in the horse-box had shown he was fine with smooth walls. The heavy leather blanket could be pulled off as he left the stalls.

'It's all a dream, anyway,' I said, 'because even if I could make such a contraption, it would take a huge amount of leather and weigh a ton. How would you ever get it on the horse at the races?'

Geraldine looked at me and uttered the words that would change the course of racing from that point on.

'What about using carpet?' she said.

The light went on. Carpet was the answer.

We drove to a carpet store in Newmarket, bought some remnant pieces and hurried to Gibson Saddlery where I began to design the kind of covering I felt might work. To create a prototype, I asked that bits of carpet be sewn to the inside and the outside of a normal stable blanket. It would be shaped in such a way that it protected the hips and flanks of the horse. The Gibson people were very cooperative and we were back at the stable within two hours to try it out. The moment I put the blanket on Prince of Darkness, I could sense a feeling of relaxation come over him.

As soon as we began to work through the starting stall, it was obvious we had finally met his needs. I gave Geraldine a pat on the back and congratulated her for coming up with the carpet idea. We had saved this horse's career. I worked him in and out several times and was convinced we had solved the problem.

Realizing that the following day was Good Friday and shops would be closed for business, we raced back to Gibson's to modify the blanket so that it could be used at the races. Equipped with a breast collar and a ring at the back with which to pull it off when the race began, we had our design. Prince of Darkness was scheduled to race on the Monday and we had precious little time to prepare.

Sir Mark was off to France on Friday but by telephone he prevailed upon the stewards to approve the use of the carpet at Warwick racecourse. George Duffield would be the jockey and he would drive me to the races with my carpet tucked away in the boot of the car. When I met George, he seemed to be game to try this invention, but a little embarrassed.

'Carpet? He's wearing a carpet?'

'That's what it's made of, sure.'

'Is it patterned carpet, or plain?'

'It has a slight pattern, I suppose you'd say.'

'Oh no,' he groaned.

'Don't you like patterned carpet?'

George held his hands up in mock surrender.

'No…it's fine. I don't mind looking like an idiot. Maybe I ought to wear the same pattern. Let's go for it. Trade in the silks. Can we stop at a carpet shop on the way and measure me up for a tufted Wilton?'

I assured him that Prince of Darkness had to have his magic carpet or he'd refuse to start.

At Warwick, the head starter was similarly apprehensive about the blanket but Sir Mark had been given permission to use this unconventional apparatus, and the stewards couldn't back out now.

When I put the blanket up behind George, it drew a lot of comments from the other jockeys. I remember Willy Carson laughing and asking George if he planned to wear it throughout the running.

'Sure,' George replied, 'none of your horses will pass me if I make the lead wearing this thing.'

Prince of Darkness entered the stall without fuss, stood totally relaxed and when the starter pushed the button, he flew out of the stall the fastest of the eighteen horses. The blanket was left behind as planned and lay on the ground in the stall. Success!

As the horses were running, I felt an arm around my shoulders and turning I saw the smiling face of Geraldine Rees. I had no idea she'd made the trip but we were one pair of happy horsemen at that moment.

Prince of Darkness went on to be a good winner and while never a champion, he paved the way for thousands of horses to experience successful racing careers when they would otherwise not pass the first test, the starting gate. Apparently, more than 10,000 horses have used the blanket between 1990 and the time of writing.

THE OSBALDESTON HORSE

One of the cities I was scheduled to visit on a 1995 tour of England was a place called Osbaldeston, in the north. A large equestrian centre there was the venue and one of the themes of the event was problems in loading horses for transport. Often horses are treated in a very brutal way when they refuse to load and it's not necessary – I've proved this countless times, over and over.

I arrived at midday and was soon approached by a girl of around twelve years of age. She had brought a horse that was impossible to load in a trailer, she said. I asked if she was sure it was impossible and she told me she was absolutely sure. I suppose I was being facetious when I inquired, 'So, if he's impossible to load in a trailer, how did you get here?'

'I rode him,' she said. 'I rode twenty-five miles yesterday and five miles this morning. I stayed with some friends last night and got here about an hour ago.'

I was stunned. When I asked this brave little girl if she'd made the trip all by herself, she told me her mother came along in the car and checked on her from time to time, but often she rode on her own. She told me she could win with her horse in shows but she had to ride to the competitions. She explained that her father travelled a lot with his work, mostly away from England, and when he'd discovered she'd ridden for three days, staying with friends, in order to get to one competition, he was very upset. Now her horse would be destroyed if I couldn't solve this problem.

I was frozen as I contemplated the gravity of the situation. The father couldn't have known what it was like for a twelve-year-old girl to have a wonderful horse in her life and be faced with such a dilemma. I said I would do what I could. I was confident I could fix this problem and I would show her how to load the horse herself and satisfy her dad. He had every right to be concerned about her riding on the roads and I was sure he'd be fine as soon as we could train the horse to load properly.

Schooling a horse to back up comfortably while being handled from the ground is critically important to my system of dealing with a difficult loader and I asked her if her horse backed up well. She assured me that it was extremely easy to back him. I didn't go to see the horse because I never touch any of the horses I use in demonstrations until the audience is present, and I had decided to take this one for my loading demonstration. He would be the final horse of the event.

It was about ten o'clock when the bay gelding was led to the centre of my round pen. The girl took the microphone and told the audience her story. There was total silence as she described the difficulties she and her family had faced for the last three years or so. I did a join-up with the horse, which seemed to go quite well. He was following me around the pen within four or five minutes.

With my training halter in place, I began the schooling process designed to cause the horse to cooperate in such a fashion that he would lead forwards easily, stop on cue and back up without hesitation. When I got to the backing up part, he had roots in the ground. I couldn't back the horse one step, no matter what I did. The girl was sitting on a chair near the gate where the horse entered the ring and, speaking on the microphone so everyone could hear, I looked at her and said, 'This afternoon you told me your horse backed really well. Now that I'm out here trying it, I find it's next to impossible. Why did you tell me he would back up so easily?'

'If you want him to back up, Mr Roberts, take him over by that trailer and see how he backs up then,' she replied. With that, the audience roared with laughter and it took me several minutes to compose myself before continuing my work.

That, in fact, has turned out to be the primary theme of my loading demonstrations since then. When the horse owns reverse gear for himself, he can use reverse against you whenever he chooses. When reverse is owned by a partnership of man and horse, and is a direction that is executed by both members of the partnership, you remove the potential for the horse to use reverse to gain the upper hand. It was on this night and under these circumstances that I first became fully aware of this phenomenon and how important cooperative backing is in the scheme of properly training a horse.

When the laughter subsided, I continued to work with my training halter, first just to get a step or two in reverse and after about six or seven minutes achieving good cooperation. Once I could walk with the horse willingly following, stop and have the horse halt at my shoulder and then back comfortably as part of the routine, it was time to approach the trailer. I led the gelding towards it, stopping and backing up periodically as we came closer to the vehicle. My routine at this point resembled a kind of dance between the horse and me. When I felt a good level of willingness on the part of my equine student, I asked him to enter the trailer.

The horse followed me straight in. As I came out, I could see that the girl was in a state of shock. She was sitting with her mouth open and when I asked her to take the mike and respond to us, she was speechless. I loaded the horse ten or twelve times and ended the evening having the girl load him herself. She was beaming with pride as she walked her horse in and out of the trailer several times. She stopped at one point and threw her arms around his neck, with tears rolling down each cheek. She thanked me with a big hug, too.

She told me that some friends had brought a trailer with them and later I met them with the girl and her mother. The child loaded her horse probably fifteen times in their trailer before they drove off into the darkness, waving goodbye.

LOMITAS AND
THE GERMAN DYNASTY

In 1988, a German-bred mare by the name of La Colorada by Surumu gave birth to a copper chestnut colt named Lomitas, and at nineteen months of age, Lomitas was placed with Bremen racing trainer, Andreas Wohler.

Andreas knew very early that he had a talented baby on his hands, but he was very careful to limit his training as a two-year-old. Lomitas had two starts in 1990, both in the autumn, which meant he was around thirty months of age. He won both and because they were important two-year-old races, he was named the champion in that category for the 1990 season.

The horse was owned by Walther Jacobs, founder of Gestut Fahrhof of Bremen, one of Germany's leading breeding and racing establishments. Early in 1991, excitement was palpable among the Jacobs family and at the Wohler stable. They had the early favourite for the German Derby in July and it appeared that he was by far the best of his age. While Andreas knew that Lomitas was a bit of a handful at times, he was confident there would be no problem racing him in April. That confidence was shattered when Lomitas refused to enter the starting stall. A full starting crew battled with him for a very dangerous twenty minutes and eventually got him in. He went on to win easily.

Disappointed but not panicked, everyone in the organization went to work to prepare Lomitas for a test in front of the stewards, which was required because of his behaviour. While he passed, it was a pretty dodgy performance. None the less, he was cleared to travel to Cologne in May for his second race as a three-year-old.

Lomitas didn't want to load into the horse-box to travel to Cologne, and when it was time to enter the starting stall, he simply said no. With an important owner and a very important young horse, the racetrack crew gave it their best effort, but what happened on the racecourse that day defies belief.

The crew literally wrestled with Lomitas. They put a hood on to blindfold him; they yanked his tail over his back, and the jockey actually held it over his shoulder. A dozen men, some in front, some behind, alternately pulled and pushed the horse, trying to force him forwards and towards the stall. This went on, some say, for thirty minutes.

The stewards radioed to disqualify the horse; they'd run the race without him. Meanwhile, Lomitas was lying on the turf, totally exhausted from the battle. He lay like a fallen soldier, immobile and in disgrace. The race started without him.

This catastrophic incident resulted in the immediate banning of Lomitas from racing worldwide. The embarrassment for the family was overwhelming, and for Andreas Wohler it was a trainer's worst nightmare.

As Mr Jacobs left the racetrack, trainer John Gosden spoke with him. He was very upset because a horse that he'd transported from England for this race had been injured while in his starting stall during the time that the men were attempting to load Lomitas. Mr Jacobs could only apologize.

'You need Monty Roberts,' John Gosden said.

Somehow, Mr Jacobs remembered the name. He called Andreas Wohler the next day to request that contact be made and on 12 June 1991, I put my life on hold and left for Germany. At Bremen airport a young man in riding breeches was waiting, perhaps a lad who'd been sent to meet me.

'Do you know Andreas Wohler?' I asked.

'I'm Andreas Wohler,' he said.

We drove immediately to the Bremen racecourse where Andreas operates his training stable for up to a hundred Thoroughbred racehorses. What happened next in my life takes its place along with my memories of Ginger and Brownie, my marriage to Pat, the birth of our children, my days with Johnny Tivio and my first meeting with Queen Elizabeth. There'd be a time before Lomitas and a time after him.

When I entered his box stall, he turned his head to look at me. Out loud and filled with awe, I said the single word, 'Gorgeous!' This chestnut Thoroughbred

A terrible time in his life: Lomitas is disqualified from racing, Cologne, Germany, May 1991

stallion stood 16.0 hands and weighed about 1,150 pounds. He had a white pastern on the off hind leg and a star between his eyes with an elongated strip that widened and ended between his nostrils. Every point of his skeletal frame hit its mark, creating the near perfect racehorse conformation.

I walked over to where he was munching his hay, and stood against the back of his stall to greet him with a stroke on his neck. 'Hello, Lomitas, you're a fine man, eh?' I proceeded to move my hands back along his body and I felt he wanted to push into my hands, away from the wall. I held out against the pressure and he immediately kicked out. I logged this as a possible response to any number of things and continued making his acquaintance. He struck me as a breathtaking animal with a look in his eye that spoke of very high intelligence.

I had travelled a long way to be standing here and suddenly I felt very pleased to have made the journey. My task was specific – cure this horse of his starting stall phobia.

After my first phone call with Andreas, he had constructed a solid wall, permanent training stall, which was much safer than the conventional kind. I had also asked for an assistant who could speak English and knew horses well. Naturally, if I were to train someone to work with Lomitas in my absence, he would also have to speak German to be effective. Andreas introduced me to a young man by the name of Simon Stokes. Simon, originally from England, was a steeplechase jockey, who at that point was considering retirement from jump racing.

While I didn't know it at the time, Simon Stokes would prove to be a champion the equal of Lomitas himself. Simon and his wife Cordula and daughter Celine would eventually become as close to Pat and me as immediate family. Simon had everything I needed. He was bi-lingual and full of experience that would prove to be invaluable in meeting the challenge that lay ahead of us.

On the first day, I took Lomitas to a small covered exercise track, not much more than a hallway that allowed for all-weather training. I led Lomitas into the structure and backed to a point near the end of the lead rope. I asked him to step towards me but he seemed very reluctant to cooperate. I raised one arm sharply above my head and then the other. He didn't seem unduly alarmed, which told me that he probably hadn't been abused with whips.

Evidence was mounting that Lomitas's primary problem was claustrophobia. Although his relationship with humans was obviously good, he was prepared to blame us for placing him in tight areas. I stopped for a moment to allow the two of us a breather. I remember stepping away from him, looking him over and thinking out loud, 'I am in the presence of greatness. I had better do my job with patience, diligence and competence.'

Testing Lomitas for signs of abuse was not because I distrusted Andreas or Simon, but I always accord my horses the respect of asking them to speak for themselves. I have been lied to by some people but never by a horse. It's not in their make-up. It is also the case that people will often tell you what they believe to be the truth, while the horse sees the facts in an entirely different way. Most people will try to give you a straight story but many fail to assess their horse's version.

I led Lomitas back to a spot near his stable and was walking him in circles, getting to know him, when Andreas and Simon returned. I gave them a short report on my get-acquainted session and asked Andreas if there was a round pen or lungeing ring nearby. I told him I needed to turn Lomitas loose before I could gain his trust. Andreas had no idea of my working methods and had never heard of join-up. With a minute to think, he remembered a show-jumping ring about ten miles away, but this would mean loading Lomitas and was probably out of the question.

'No,' I replied. 'If he doesn't want to go on the truck, that will be part of our training programme.'

Both Andreas and Simon were very nervous about this idea but in the end they telephoned the transport company and soon we had a beautiful horse-box at our disposal. Andreas suggested backing it into the barn with the ramp in the centre aisle. He told me they had done this before, using horse blankets to frighten him on to the truck.

A wonderful time in his life: Lomitas wins in Germany, June 1991

'He's going to have to learn to load like a gentleman if I'm to work with him,' I said. 'I'll school him with my training halter, and then we'll ask him to load.'

Lomitas was a very good student and quickly learned to respect both the halter and me. I decided that, until he caused me a problem, I was going to treat him like a normal horse, including loading into the van.

After a few minutes' work with the halter, I walked up the ramp and he willingly followed me. The instant he was inside, the helpers standing outside ran to lift the ramp.

'No,' I told them. 'Leave the ramp down. I'm going to walk him off and on several times.'

Some Irish exercise riders called out to me, 'If you bring him off, you'll never get him back on again.'

I asked them to have faith and walked Lomitas off and on the van without incident fifteen to twenty times before we closed it up and drove away, with the lads watching in disbelief. I chose to ride in the back of the truck, so I could get an idea of how my young horse handled circumstances that might cause his adrenaline to rise. He seemed fine and we made the trip to the show-jumping yard without any trouble. When the horse-box was stopped at the new location, I led him off and on the van several times.

Andreas, Simon and I used jump poles to fashion a sort of round pen approximately fifty feet in diameter in one corner of the show-jumping arena. The doors were closed so, even if he jumped out, Lomitas would be confined to the building and was in no danger. Then I went to work.

I released Lomitas, allowing him the freedom to canter away from me. Within a minute or two, he was giving me all the signals I look for before asking a horse to join-up with me. When the time was right, I went through the appropriate gestures, inviting him to come to the centre of the pen and be with me. This was an intelligent horse and in a very few minutes I had a successful join-up, and he was in full conversation with me.

Now I wanted to take this trust a bit further. We dismantled our make-believe round pen and allowed Lomitas the freedom of the full arena. He immediately ran from me and seemed intent upon taking charge, dictating what our relationship should be. After about five minutes, I was able to convey to him that it was better to be my partner than an adversary. I used no violence. Through communication, he was now following me everywhere I went.

I began to feel a level of confidence that was ultra satisfying as I showed Andreas and Simon the principles involved in gaining the trust of your horse. After less than an hour of schooling at the show-jumping facility, we were ready to load up again for the return trip. Andreas and Simon stiffened and prepared for trouble when it was time to load but Lomitas stayed relaxed and walked on without hesitation.

I slept well that night, feeling good about my chances of success. I had overcome several obstacles that had spelled danger for my horse during this critical time of training.

The following day I began to work with Lomitas at the permanent training stall. I was banking on the trust I had created the day before and soon I had him going in and out with no problems. Later in the morning, when Simon had finished his regular duties, I asked him to put some tack on our horse. While he sat on Lomitas, I continued to lead him in and out of the stall. Before we finished that morning, I was able to close the gate behind him and get him to walk out the front in a very relaxed manner. These lessons meant we had bridged another gap on our way to solving his starting-stall phobia.

That afternoon the head starter from the Bremen racecourse, Herr Dunker, dropped by to check on Lomitas's progress. He spoke very little English but I could tell that he was sceptical where Lomitas was concerned. However, he agreed to recommend that the starters allow Lomitas to have another test on the racecourse to assess the possibility of lifting his ban.

The following morning, 16 June, a group of five racing officials gathered on the Bremen racecourse at about eleven and I brought Lomitas to a set of regulation stalls, which were placed on the turf near the official racing surface. Terry Hellier, the primary jockey for Andreas Wohler at that time, was up. I must say he was a brave young man and stayed calm through the entire procedure. Lomitas entered the gate, stood relatively quietly and broke acceptably.

The stewards were impressed but quick to point out that I had worked with him for a couple of days only. They wanted to see another test before the ban was lifted. Lomitas had performed alone that morning and the stewards said they wanted the next test to include horses on either side of him. It was arranged for 18 June and Andreas targeted a race for 23 June.

I schooled Lomitas the next day and felt he had decidedly improved on his performance in front of the stewards. The eighteenth proved to be a glorious day for my chestnut horse as he passed his test with flying colours. The stewards reinstated him but for one race only because they knew how dangerous he could be. They wanted me to bring him to the start personally and no racetrack employees were to be allowed to handle him. That suited me just fine.

On the morning of the race I was as tense as I have ever been under similar circumstances. There were nearly 20,000 fans at the racecourse and it seemed that every one of them was looking straight at Lomitas and me as we walked towards the starting stalls. Lomitas had become a sort of folk hero to German racing fans. Parents held children over the rail and they called out, 'Lomie, Lomie, Lomie.'

The stewards had agreed I would be the last to load my horse and furthermore they had given me ten minutes maximum to get the job done. As I walked Lomitas in circles behind the stalls, I realized that something was wrong. All of the other jockeys and horses were gathered on the far side of the track. Trainers were there, too, and they appeared to be having some sort of meeting. Andreas came across the track.

'They want to boycott the race unless Lomitas goes in first,' he said, 'so they can see that he's OK before they have to enter and wait for him.'

'Let's go,' I said. 'I'll go in first.'

'Are you crazy?' said Andreas. 'We have permission to go in last, and it'll be much harder to load him with no horses in there.'

With that, I went to my assigned gate and walked straight in with Lomitas accompanying me quietly. The head starter shouted to the rest of the jockeys and they loaded their horses immediately while Lomitas stood there calmly. Ironically, track officials had considerable difficulties with some of the other horses. Finally, all were in and Lomitas broke well with the field. He lay in third spot for most of the race and then simply overwhelmed the field in the last quarter of a mile. It was an incredible pleasure to see him take his rightful place in the winner's circle.

This triumph was the first in a series of victories for Lomitas. Later that year, he was named Germany's champion three-year-old and horse of the year. I travelled to Germany often throughout 1991 to assist in Lomitas's races but Simon Stokes did my work most of the time. He became very good at handling Lomitas and because of this association was eventually offered the job of racing manager for Gestut Fahrhof, a position he has held for over ten years. He is now a licensed trainer.

Lomitas went on to amass a record that, in my opinion, is more important than any other racehorse I've dealt with. He didn't win the most money but with three Group I races to his credit and horse of the year honours, he surpasses even Alleged as my favourite racehorse of all time. Lomitas won ten races, had three seconds and one third, collecting $918,656.

Lomitas's second life at stud may prove even more important than his first life as a racehorse. He's now a champion sire and, from his first crop, produced the winner of the 1999 Group I German Derby, champion three-year-old and horse of the year Belenus. To date, Lomitas's offspring have won nearly $8,000,000.

Lomitas after retirement

I encouraged Sheikh Mohammed bin Rashid al Maktoum of Dubai, the world's leading owner, to buy breeding rights to Lomitas and he responded by buying seven lifetime spots. Lomitas is now standing in Newmarket to a full book of about eighty mares and, because of the involvement of Sheikh Mohammed, seven are from the world's leading broodmare band.

However, the true satisfaction I derived from my experience with Lomitas comes from the close emotional attachment I formed with him. I use the word 'great' very seldom but I attach it to Lomitas with confidence. He was great. It's not likely I will work with another horse that achieves so much. To have done so is a privilege I will cherish for the rest of my days.

After my successful work with Lomitas, Walther Jacobs asked me to become a consultant to his operation and to take charge of starting each of his babies before they were sent to the racing stables. I was pleased to take on both of these roles and, of all the good fortune I've had in the racing industry, I feel that my accomplishments with Gestut Fahrhof are the most significant of my career. The team and I have worked together on many horses since Lomitas, including eight champions, and I hope we'll enjoy many more.

The first group of American yearlings I sent to Fahrhof included Quebrada, by Devil's Bag out of Queen to Conquer. The second group included Risen Raven, by Risen Star out of Aurania, and then came Macanal, by Northern Flagship out of Magnala. These three all became champions and high earners.

Simon and I have started over three hundred young Thoroughbreds for Fahrhof. Of these, six went on to become classic winners, thirty-nine were Group winners (in internationally approved Group stakes races) with fifty-six listed winners (in internationally approved stakes races). Lavirco and Suraco, both foaled in 1993, finished first and second in the 1996 German Derby and Suraco went on to win $1,020,000.

One of my early tasks for Walther Jacobs was to buy a group of broodmares for Lomitas. When I found Spirit of Eagles, I wrote on her pedigree the word 'sprinter' because she ran most of her races at six furlongs (1,200 metres). I liked her conformation and the fact that she was very sound with fifty-nine starts in her racing career. In 1996, when bred to Lomitas, she produced Silvano. He won his only start as a two-year-old. The next year he raced five

CLOCKWISE FROM TOP *Macanal, Lavirco and Risen Raven*

times, winning twice including a Group II race, and at four, he raced four times, each one a Group race, and was in the money every time.

In 2001, Silvano really hit his stride. He won the Group I Singapore Cup, breaking a track record. He also won the Group I Arlington Million in Chicago and the Group II Queen Elizabeth II Cup as well as coming second in the Group I Man o' War Stakes in New York. He was named Germany's horse of the year and, with career earnings of $2,321,024, he was retired to stud for 2002 with an international rating of 121.

Sabiango, a foal of 1999, is another son of Spirit of Eagles, this time by Acatenango, who stands at stud at Gestut Fahrhof. Although he was already a Group I winner, he seemed to be going backwards in his form in late 2003.

OPPOSITE *Spirit of Eagles*
BELOW *Silvano at the Sha Tin racecourse for the Hong Kong Invitational*
(*Queen Elizabeth II Cup*) *in 2001. The jockey is Andreas Suborics*

Sabiango

In the New Year, an agreement was made with Andreas Jacobs to allow me to bring Sabiango to California to race. I made the decision to put him with a young trainer, Tim Yakteen, who works under Bob Baffert. I knew Tim from the time he worked under another all-time great trainer, Charlie Whittingham. I had the feeling that Tim could bring this horse back to his winning ways. Tim took his charge under his wing and found Sabiango to exhibit outstanding athletic ability and a willingness to work.

In early April 2004, we decided to point Sabiango towards the $350,000 Charlie Whittingham Memorial Handicap at Hollywood Park on 12 June. Despite a minor setback caused by a virus, he was entered and ready to run on the day. To everyone's delight, Sabiango, ridden by 21-year-old jockey Tyler Baze, won the Group I race wire to wire in a stunning victory. It was an emotional moment for all of us in the winner's circle, but for Tim it was also hugely poignant: he'd won the race named for and honouring his friend and mentor. Time will tell what the future has in store for this outstanding young runner.

Sabiango's dam, Spirit of Eagles, was named broodmare of the world for 2001. That same year, Fahrhof purchased a yearling at auction, a chestnut filly called Royal Dubai, by Dashing Blade out of Reem Dubai. In 2002 she became the eighth champion produced by Fahrhof since I joined them in 1991.

Walther Jacobs' grandson, Dr Andreas Jacobs, is now chairman of the board and he issued the following statement:

> The year 2001 has been the most significant in the racing history of Gestut Fahrhof. Our breeding and racing programme has attained new heights on a broader international scale than I could have dreamed possible. Victory in the Arlington Million has rewritten the record books of Gestut Fahrhof. Monty Roberts saved the racing career of Lomitas and then brought us Spirit of Eagles and several other fine young mares. Monty started Silvano and Sabiango as well as virtually all of the youngsters Fahrhof has produced. Fahrhof is the result of a team effort and right from foaling time there are many people who give their energy to the production of fine racehorses. Simon Stokes, our racing manager, and Andreas Wohler, the trainer of both Silvano and Sabiango, should also be mentioned as contributing greatly to the success of our programme.

I thank the Jacobs family for their confidence.

Gestut Fahrhof has been a dream come true for me. My association with this operation has allowed me to use my life's experiences with some of the best breeding in Europe. It's so much fun for me to spend about a month each year working with wonderful young Thoroughbreds and doing it from daylight to dark. The opportunity to work alongside Simon Stokes has afforded me the chance to pass on the knowledge I have gathered from the tens of thousands of horses I have dealt with over the past decades. I am one of the few people on earth who has had the opportunity to learn from the American mustangs that can be acquired for $125 and then work with virtually every breed.

The brain of equus is a fertile pool of information whether in the head of a mustang or a racing Thoroughbred valued at tens of millions of dollars. Each day of my life I am grateful for the chances I have had to experience horses across the broadest base of disciplines. I hope the concepts that I've discovered will be carried forward so as to create a deeper understanding between man and horse.

DAYFLOWER,
LA CONFEDERATION
AND SONG OF AFRICA

After Prince of Darkness and Lomitas, the horse network zeroed in on me as someone who could mend problem horses. We were receiving four or five calls a week from all over the world and I had to pick and choose because there were simply not enough squares on the calendar to deal with all of them.

One day I got a call from Henry Cecil. He had a filly in training at Warren Hill with a serious aversion to the starting stalls. She belonged to Sheikh Mohammed and she was one of his favourite Thoroughbreds. Henry said that Sheikh Mohammed was asking a special favour of me, to go and work with her.

Sheikh Mohammed probably owns more Thoroughbreds than anyone else, and he certainly leads the world if monetary value is the criterion. He also owns hundreds of Arab horses of the highest quality and even some top-notch Quarter Horses. He's a serious horseman, taking part in high-level endurance competitions and being involved with his own race training. There are many facets to this man – his falcons, his camels, his architectural achievements and even his deep understanding of the business world – but I view him first and foremost as a horseman of the highest calibre.

The filly in question was called Dayflower. I recall as if it were yesterday standing in the middle of Henry Cecil's large walking circle behind the stables. From the north end, through an opening in a hedge, the filly appeared, led by assistant Steven Dible, with Henry walking along behind. I believe I must

A winning day for Dayflower in England

have felt a lot like Prince Rainier of Monaco when he first laid eyes on Grace Kelly, spellbound by the beauty and regal bearing of this gorgeous creature.

'How is she bred?' I asked Henry, and he told me that she was by Majestic Light out of Equate by Raja Baba.

Dayflower walked in a most effortless way and seemed to be totally at ease with her surroundings. Steven, better known by his nickname, Yarmie, stopped her, and she looked over at me with two of the most beautiful eyes I have ever seen on a horse – large, black and doe-like.

Henry told me they had managed to get her in my solid, wooden training stall a few times, but the regulation metal stalls seemed to be certain death as far as she was concerned. He told me he had never before seen a horse so frightened of the starting stalls, and Henry had seen a lot of horses in his time.

I asked Yarmie to lead Dayflower around the stable to an area where we could see the regulation stalls. He said he'd have to remain about 100 yards, or metres, from them because she had become so phobic about the sight of them.

When we rounded the end of the row of stables and came into view of the stalls, Dayflower stopped in her tracks. Her ears up and eyes intently fixed on the stalls, she began to quiver as if the temperature had dropped below freezing. Soon her whole body was in a state of spasm. Her skin bounced up and down as if she was standing on a vibrator, causing an uncontrollable shaking of her entire anatomy.

Then I saw something I had never seen before, or since. Huge droplets of perspiration seemed to rise to the tips of her dry hair. Dayflower's hair was standing on end, like many horses' coats will do in cold weather, and then these large balls of sweat began to roll off. After two to three minutes, Dayflower was as wet as if she had been given a full bath. The sight was shocking. This would be a daunting challenge.

Taking her to their round pen, I did my initial join-up work with Dayflower and schooled her in a training halter. I spent more than an hour that afternoon just trying to get her somewhere near the stalls that frightened her so, and I began to sense that she was happier if the stalls were up against a solid wall. With the wall on one side, she had less freedom to take flight in a way that was dangerous to her.

Over the next few days I worked with Dayflower for many hours and managed to convince her that the stalls wouldn't kill her and, eventually, she handled them with poise. We progressed to the racecourse stalls and, because of the foundation we had laid down, she handled them well after just two sessions.

I left Dayflower in the care of Henry Cecil's staff. Yarmie had worked with me on several remedial horses before and he did a good job continuing my work after I had gone. She remained one of Sheikh Mohammed's favourites and while she never won any classic races, she did win four times, earning a total of $81,048.

I didn't realize it at the time, but Dayflower had made a significant impact. In making her request for the solid wall to help her overcome her extreme fear of the stalls, she enabled me to help literally thousands of other horses with a similar fear. A dark bay filly called La Confederation and another mare, Song of Africa, extended the lesson.

When I first heard about La Confederation, the story I was told made my blood run cold. Anthony Stroud called me on behalf of Sheikh Mohammed and I cleared the calendar, catching the first flight to Paris en route to Chantilly and the stables of one of Europe's leading Thoroughbred trainers, André Fabre.

At Charles de Gaulle airport I was met by one of André Fabre's exercise riders. Fluent in French, even though his first language was English, the young man was wearing a cowboy hat. I called him Tex.

Tex was also a travelling lad and, on the way to Chantilly, he told me he had been assigned to the project so he could learn the ropes but, in his opinion, nothing could be done for this filly. She had shown some talent in her speed tests but, according to Tex, her brain was put in backwards when God made her. They had around two hundred horses in training and none of the others had problems like this filly had. He believed it was simply the way she was wired and had nothing to do with the environment or her experiences.

Apparently, the only way they could get La Confederation in her box stall was to put a pungent substance in her nose to take away her ability to smell, blindfold her and at a fair distance from the stable, spin her in circles so as to disorient her. Approaching the stall, several lads would assist the groom by locking arms behind her and bracing from each side, literally pushing her through the door.

Tex went on to say the same process had to be gone through to get her out of the stall, and as far as transportation was concerned, there was no way to load her short of using heavy tranquillizers and many men to push her on. They had attempted the starting stall once but it was a frightening experience, with the rider down and the filly running through the forest to get away from the apparatus she so feared.

Driving into Chantilly is an experience for any horseman to savour. It stands alone as the most beautiful training ground anywhere in the world. Hundreds of years old, the training tracks are carved out of forests that were standing before horses were domesticated. As we drove by the lake and the chateau, I remembered the story of the former ruler of this area. He'd left his tiny kingdom to the government of France with the provision it would forever remain training grounds for horses. It is said he believed in reincarnation. He would come back as a racehorse and wanted to live in his beloved Chantilly. La Confederation was the eighth or tenth horse I had worked on here, and both Pat and I had come to love the place.

By the time we arrived at the training stables, I must admit I was extremely concerned about whether or not I could do anything for this deeply troubled filly. It was close to noon when I first saw her and she seemed perfectly normal as she munched on some hay in a spacious stall that was a part of a stone stable, more than one hundred years old. I stepped inside and observed a dark bay filly, quite attractive athletically speaking. While not as beautiful as Dayflower, I could easily see why Sheikh Mohammed's team had advised her purchase.

André Fabre's yard was as beautiful as any I had ever seen. Six separate stone buildings housed the horses. Each one was set up with thirty to forty box stalls and each one might have won an architectural award at some time. The surfaces in and around the buildings were works of art, cobblestones laid in traditional European patterns. The walkways for the horses were about twelve feet wide with a deep cushion of shredded bark, creating a safe surface for the horses to walk on.

Escorting me to a spacious office, Tex introduced me to André Fabre, who was poring over charts of the day's workouts. He was obviously very busy and our meeting was brief and to the point. André told me that Sheikh Mohammed had great confidence in my work and felt I could cure the filly of her phobias.

However, he emphasized that he had never encountered quite such a troubled young Thoroughbred and if I simply could not see a way to change her, to let him know as soon as possible so he could communicate this to the Sheikh.

Tex took me to a small café where many of the exercise riders had lunch. I felt very strange being in the presence of so many people talking about horses and yet understanding hardly a word of what they said. He told me that La Confederation was the topic of conversation throughout Chantilly. Virtually every lad and lass had an opinion one way or another about whether I could solve her problems. Apparently, most of them thought I had no chance.

We were back at the yard by one-thirty and I checked the equipment that had been ordered for me. The custom-made blanket that had been sent by Gibson Saddlery seemed to be just fine. I fitted protective leg boots to my filly, who stood quite comfortably while I put them on her, and checked the special halters I had brought with me to be sure they were the right size.

My first goal was to convince La Confederation that she should walk quietly in and out of her box stall. She had obviously never been trained to back up well from the ground and I must have worked for twenty minutes or so on practically nothing else. I then put the special protective blanket on her and within five minutes or so she was comfortable wearing it as I walked her, stopped her and backed her up, all within the confines of her stall. When she backed up with ease, I began to back her towards the door, instead of trying to move through it in the conventional manner. 'That's a girl, Connie,' I told her, as she managed to get her hind legs on to the cobblestones just outside her stable. Tex and I had shortened her name to Connie.

I suppose I worked for about an hour, after which I could back Connie out of the stall, continue to ask her to back up, negotiate a circle and back her into the stall. Tex was quite amazed and I had him take a turn to get a feel for the halter. Within an hour and half, I was walking her forward in and out of her box stall, taking a few steps at a time.

Throughout the training session, Connie was sending a signal that she'd hit her hip on the wooden frame of the door at some point, and that's what set up the phobia about the door. I deduced that the pain had created a fear that had spilled over to encompass the starting stalls and transport vehicle as well. When I had Connie right, she was totally relaxed and comfortable following me, with a low pulse rate and a very acceptable adrenaline level.

It must have been around five-thirty when I said that Connie had had enough. Tex set up her feed in her box stall and I led her inside, taking everything off. First, I removed the blanket as she was reaching for her grain tub. Next, I stripped off the halter and she dug right in. Her disposition stayed sweet as I removed the four protective leg boots.

We had been allowing Connie to drink occasionally throughout the afternoon and it was a good sign to see her appetite so keen. We left the box stall with our filly eating up a storm. When a Thoroughbred backs away from food, it is often because of nervous tension, particularly with a filly. Eating in this way told us she was not traumatized by the long schooling session I had given her.

Leaving the stable, Tex walked me to the horse-box that was to be our schoolroom the following morning. Equipped with state-of-the-art safety features, it was painted in the colours of André Fabre, with notices asking drivers to be aware that it carried racing Thoroughbreds.

After I had given the truck a good inspection, Tex walked me a short way through beautiful, old growth trees to a clearing where a permanent training stall had been constructed for my work. It was the same design as the one in Henry Cecil's yard, where I had schooled Prince of Darkness, Dayflower and many others. Near the permanent wooden training stall was a round pen about sixty feet in diameter. It looked as though it had been there for many decades and had probably been used as a lungeing ring or turn out in the past. Tex told me the regulation training stalls were about half a mile away in a forested area.

Tex drove me to the Alibird Hotel, about three miles from the stable, where I was to stay, arranging to pick me up at six in the morning. I told Tex I thought it would take at least four, and possibly six, days to accomplish my goals. I don't know why I gave him those numbers because, at that time, I knew nothing of the depth of Connie's aversion to the starting stalls. While I had confidence that we would be able to load her comfortably into the truck the following morning, it was the starting stall that was haunting me.

Back at the stables early next morning, we found that Connie had finished her breakfast and seemed to be feeling well. I gave her a little refresher course with that evil stall door and she passed her tests in fifteen or twenty minutes. With Tex following along, I led Connie towards the horse-box and, oh boy, was she upset when she caught sight of it!

The truck was placed on good footing. Connie was wearing her boots, her blanket and a head protector in case she reared while inside, and my halter was in place. The horse-box was a major hassle for her for about half an hour and then, with some wings – fence-like panels – on the ramp and a wall behind her, she agreed to make the trip up and into the truck. Connie was very intelligent and once the phobia was cracked, she was in and out with no problem.

My confidence was soaring. It was around eight on the morning of my first full day and I felt as though I had overcome many of the psychological problems I had travelled halfway around the world to deal with. I never had a scratch on my filly and two of her three major phobias were behind her. Eight-thirty was a breakfast break for the exercise riders and Tex and I took Connie back to her stall, stripped her down and decided we would give her an hour to eat, drink and rest.

It was about nine-thirty when we went back and suited her up again for her late morning schooling session. Taking a halter, four protective boots and a thirty-foot driving line, we trekked through the trees to the area where the round pen was located. Once in the pen, I did a join-up session with Connie. She was very communicative and exhibited a high level of intelligence. Within fifteen minutes, she was following me wherever I went and seemed happy to be with me.

Tex brought the protective blanket into the pen and placed it on Connie. As she had already worn it in the stable, she accepted it straight away. I schooled her with the training halter, forward, stop, back and turn, left and right. She was fully cooperative as I led her from the ring towards the training stall. With total confidence, I walked up behind the stall and began my normal procedures to ask her to enter the narrow structure. I believe it was about my second or third request when Connie stood on her hind legs and struck out over the line.

The instant Connie had a front leg over the line, she knew she was in full control. Whirling away from us, she immediately fled as fast as she could. I had to let go of the thirty-foot line and stood frozen in my tracks, paralyzed with fear. With the blanket waving on her flanks, Connie ran through the trees like a deer in full flight, thirty feet of line waving behind her and threatening to wrap around a tree or a bush with every stride she took. My heart was in my mouth. I didn't think she could negotiate the hundred yards back to the stable without hitting a tree, which was likely to injure her severely or even cause death. What happened next was one of life's most memorable moments. La Confederation did not touch a tree. She ran straight to her box stall, somehow crossing over the cobblestones and passing through the door without so much as a hesitation. This was the same door she'd refused to walk through just two days before.

Both Tex and I were running towards the stable as fast as our legs could carry us and I listened for a moment for sounds that might come from inside the stall. My thought was she had to have hit the back wall, having negotiated the door at full speed. Tex, thirty years my junior and fit as a trout, arrived while I was only about halfway there and I remember slowing down and listening for some report from him as I approached the stable. I heard him say that she was OK.

At that moment I wanted a chance to deal with every atheist on earth. I wanted to ask them how they could ever maintain that what we had just seen could happen without a God in heaven. We walked around the box stall for a few minutes and if she had hit the wall at the back of the stall, there appeared to be no ill effects. Once she settled, she looked for all the world exactly as she had done before the incident occurred.

I stripped Connie down and Tex gave her a sponge bath. We allowed her some time to drink and eat a bit of hay. Meanwhile, Tex and I talked about our next move.

'I want some livestock panels, like the ones we used as wings earlier this morning while schooling at the van. We had four of them near the truck but I'll need eight when I'm ready for my next session.'

Tex told me that would be no problem and he would see to it they were near the stall by one o'clock.

Back at the riders' café for lunch, La Confederation and I were once again the subject of heated conversation between the lads and lasses. Bets were now being laid, and Tex was acting as translator and filling me in on the discussions as best he could. I had gone from severely concerned to highly confident and back again in one twenty-four-hour period and, even though I was pleased with the stall door and the horse-box, I had nearly returned to square one. While I choked down a sandwich, Tex told me that from the beginning he'd felt I would probably get the stall and the truck done, but seriously doubted there was any way we could succeed with the starting gate.

Just after one, I walked Connie back to the area of the permanent training stall and Tex followed with the blanket. At the rear end of the stall we had created an enclosure with four of the eight livestock panels. The other four made a similar enclosure in front of the wooden structure. I waited until I had entered the rear enclosure to put the blanket on. Should La Confederation somehow get loose again, our enclosures would prevent another death-defying trip through the trees. There was no way out. The only passageway was through the stall.

It was quite a maze, this hourglass-like set up, but I was very pleased to know that my filly was safe. Connie was a basket case when asked to pass through the stall but, just as the stable door was conquered, so did we emerge victorious over the training stall. I stopped for a moment to thank Dayflower for the lesson she'd taught me, which prompted me to use this panel system. By 3.30 or so, I could walk Connie calmly through the stall, and even back her through it, accomplishing this while standing six to eight feet in front of her. This allowed her to think quietly through the act of walking or backing through the pair of wooden walls.

The goal for day three was to re-establish her confidence in the training stall, with her tack in place, a task we accomplished before the breakfast break. The café conversations were vastly different from those taking place twenty-four hours earlier. I still couldn't understand any French but a handshake and a slap on the back mean about the same all over the world.

Tex was cautious. He reminded me that the regulation starting stall was still waiting in the forest, about half a mile away.

After breakfast, I put Tex up on La Confederation and her progress was dramatic. He was able to walk her through the wooden stall, stand her in it with both gates closed and even back her in without a problem. The next step was to open the enclosures and work once again from the ground without a rider, and we finished the third day with Tex up and no support from the panels. When we had Connie standing quietly in the stall with the gates closed in front and behind, we stroked her and talked to her, and we could see an obvious increase in her comfort levels. The training stall was becoming a safe place in her mind.

At dawn on day four, Tex and I made a tour through the forest to examine the regulation starting stall. Finding no particular surprises, I suggested that we repeat each of our procedures once more before lunch, and plan to go to the metal gate in the afternoon. The morning went beautifully. Connie performed each of our early procedures without a glitch.

Scepticism was still apparent at the lunch café because most of the riders felt the regulation gate was the major hurdle to overcome. We had another rider with us on a quiet saddle horse for company when we approached the metal gate in the woods. What would she think?

No way was this filly going anywhere near the dreaded regulation stalls! She flew into a rage and while Tex stayed on board, I'm not sure how. She scored ten out of ten for danger to herself. Tex faced almost certain injury and she very nearly decapitated me with a front foot. It was clear that we required another step in the transition to the regulation gate, so it was back to the drawing board. I asked Tex to jump down and we walked back towards the stable leading her.

Then I had a thought. What if we had a tractor come and pull the regulation stalls from where they were to a point just in front of the training stall? I knew I could control Connie in the wooden structure. If I could get her to stand quietly inside and then open the gate, I might cause her to walk forward out of the training stall straight into the metal one. We would reconstruct the two circular enclosures at either end and this time the front one would sit just ahead of the regulation gate. This would ensure a safe environment once again. The lessons of Prince of Darkness, Dayflower and many others were bouncing through my brain at a mile a minute.

It worked. Within half an hour or so, we had Connie walking through both the wooden and metal stalls with Tex on her back. We finished day four executing this procedure fifty to sixty times. I often tell my students that there is no such thing as failure. Those experiences that appear to be failure are opportunities to learn. I simply needed to find the environment Connie required, and she was enlightening me with every step. Before this session concluded, Connie stood relaxed inside the metal stall while we stroked her once again and told her how wonderful she was. I explained to Tex that all horses fear the unfamiliar but seldom do they fear something they fully understand, so long as it doesn't hurt them.

Day five was dedicated to separating the metal structure from the wooden one, very gradually. We moved the regulation stall away from the wooden one, four to five feet at a time. At first, we used panels to create a hallway between the two structures, and by the end of the day, we could ride La Confederation straight into the regulation stalls. Many of the riders came round to watch the proceedings in amazement.

On day six, we asked La Confederation to accept the regulation stalls in their original position, half a mile away in the woods. We took some time to school her without a rider but, eventually, we were successful. Tex could ride her in and out of the stalls, we could close them up and even put the saddle horse in beside her. I was sore and beat up at the end of all this but the satisfaction I felt for the accomplishments achieved overrode everything.

On the afternoon of the seventh day, André Fabre rode a saddle horse through the woods to the regulation starting stalls and watched as La Confederation quietly walked in and out of the stalls, first with me leading and then entirely on her own. She was wearing her training halter and her protective blanket. Four other Thoroughbreds were ridden from the training yard to our location and the five horses were loaded into the stalls just the way it would be done at the races. Two horses were placed on each side of La Confederation and a couple of them acted up. Connie stood calmly and when the gates opened, she raced up the course, leading the other four. There was a pride-filled lump in my throat as I watched our filly. The five horses flew up the beautiful training track, making no sound as they galloped over a surface created by centuries of fallen leaves.

We had a little party at the riders' café that evening and you can't imagine the carryings on. Tex was overjoyed and he made sure the rest of the party knew it. I left the following morning, confident that La Confederation would be a successful racehorse.

About a month later, I received a call at Flag Is Up Farms from a former student of mine, Rupert Pritchard-Gordon. He was at the track and Tex was there with him, reporting that La Confederation had just raced and won easily.

I was delighted. It was no surprise to me that she could run but to have your equine student come through all those phobias and graduate with an easy win at a major French track was gratifying to the tenth power. I congratulated Tex, asking him to keep me informed about Connie's progress.

About a month after that, I received another call from Rupert. This one was very different from the first.

'It was horrible, Monty,' he said. 'She didn't want to enter the gate, and then when she did, she fought while inside. She eventually stood on her hind legs and bashed the gates open with her front feet, throwing the jockey into them. He was injured and she broke free and ran up the racecourse. She was disqualified and is now suspended from racing.'

Words can't describe how I felt after this conversation. I could not imagine what had happened to cause such a relapse in a filly as intelligent as La Confederation. I immediately called Anthony Stroud in Sheikh Mohammed's office and told him I wanted the racetrack videotape of the incident sent to me by courier as soon as possible so that I could assess the circumstances surrounding the disaster. I had the tape within three days.

When I saw what was on the official track video, I felt anger stronger than I can remember at any other time in my life. The tape clearly showed La Confederation being led towards the starting stalls with no protective blanket on, and my special training halter had been put on upside down. Her handler was a man I didn't recognize. As she approached the gate, Connie was reluctant to go near it without her blanket in place. A race attendant appeared with a long buggy whip and several men restrained her as she was whipped across the hind legs. They got her in the stall but as soon as the rails touched her flanks, the same way the stable door and the truck had done, she flew into a rage.

I could see La Confederation kick out and then rear, striking the gates open. She flew out of the metal contraption and up the racecourse running for her very life. I saw them remove the injured jockey from the stalls and take him away. I sat with a blank screen on the television when the tape was complete, trying to control the anger welling up inside me. I called Anthony Stroud and reported what I'd seen. I told him I would never go near another horse of theirs if they didn't remove La Confederation from France immediately and get her to Newmarket where she could be placed with someone who would follow my procedures to the letter.

With that conversation behind me, I called Rupert, who had by this time become well aware of the circumstances surrounding the incident. Rupert told me that the decision was made to run Connie on that particular day and, as it happened, Tex was on holiday. Others in the stable said she was doing so well, they were sure she'd be just fine. A totally untrained lad was assigned to take her to the starting stalls. He didn't know how to put on the halter and was unsure how to use the blanket. The conclusion was to leave the blanket off, which contributed greatly to the disaster.

This incident dramatizes what often happens when dealing with remedial horses. Some people will tend to regard horses in much the same way as they think of machinery. If it's broke, they want it fixed; when it's fixed, it's supposed to work. The people around La Confederation were lulled into a sense of security by her good behaviour.

Anthony Stroud and Sheikh Mohammed agreed at once to send La Confederation to Newmarket, where I went to work with her as soon as she was settled in her new surroundings. It took very little time to regain all the lost ground, and the proper procedures were followed throughout the balance of her career. I visited Connie several times while she was racing. She ultimately earned $119,203 and was an internationally approved Group winner in England. She retired from racing in 1995 and is currently raising babies in Kentucky.

The third of this trio of outstanding Thoroughbred females who came to me in rapid succession, Song of Africa, was in Florida when I met her, banned from racing and with several injuries to people and a destroyed starting gate to her credit. Dozens of horsemen on the Florida racing scene said this one was impossible, but the lessons of Dayflower and La Confederation carried me to a successful conclusion with her. Before she was retired as a broodmare, Song of Africa won six races, including an internationally approved stake, and amassed earnings of $223,538.

The respect I feel for horses such as Dayflower, La Confederation and Song of Africa, and the education I gained from them, is virtually impossible to measure. The horseman who fails to take advantage of the potential for learning presented by these horses is missing out on one of life's great experiences.

DUALLY

Pepinics Dually, or Dually for short, was a gem. A bay Quarter Horse of just 14.3 hands and 1,250 pounds, he was a very strong, world-class reined cow horse and Triple Crown Champion for the National Reined Cow Horse Association in 1994. He was bred by Greg Ward, with whom I was at college in the mid 1950s. I bought Dually after Greg had already shown him, but had a world of fun training him during the time when Greg and his son John won several championships with him.

My special training halter is named after him, a legacy of his importance to me. I designed it while he was my number one horse. The Dually halter is based on an old idea of Don Dodge's – Don, my former teacher, called it the come-along – and it has become a large part of my training life, assisting me and other horsemen around the world. The palomino stallion Barlet really showed me the need for a specifically designed halter. The come-along had to be fashioned from a long rope, but using it helped Barlet change from an angry, vicious stallion to a cooperative equine partner. Now there are approximately 120,000 Dually halters in existence and, when properly handled, they connect handlers and horses far more closely than other types of halter.

My first book, *The Man Who Listens to Horses*, was published in September 1996 and my British publisher asked me to do a book-launch tour. Alongside my usual demonstrations of join-up, I would be signing copies of the book, so they wanted the tour to have special impact. They'd heard me describing this Quarter Horse I had back home that I loved so much, and the idea occurred to them that

I should bring Dually along on the tour. Then as well as demonstrating join-up, I could show Dually working cattle and performing all the manoeuvres required in his discipline – sliding stops, spins and flying lead changes. They wanted the British audiences unfamiliar with Western shows and rodeo to get a glimpse of the skills we've developed in our horses in the western United States.

So we got out Dually's passport and booked his airfare. He did his quarantine and we made the trip together, although we very nearly didn't go. My doctor diagnosed a dangerous type of pneumonia and forbade me to travel. There was no way I wasn't going – this was a big moment for me. My life story was being published, I was booked in twenty cities and towns across the country, including six stops in Ireland, and Dually was ready to go. I knocked back three times the recommended dose of my prescription and boarded a KLM plane to Amsterdam.

Dually performs a beautiful stop with a loose rein, 1996. It gave me great
pleasure to ride this Triple Crown Champion Working Cow Horse

I felt so ill I couldn't sit next to another person, so I left my seat, ducked through the little door at the back and curled up next to Dually in the hold. My lungs were half full of liquid and my temperature was off the scale. I was close to passing out but I received such solace from the calm presence of Dually. We made it but it was one of the few times in my life when I had good reason to think I was going to die.

From Amsterdam, Dually and I rode a truck to Calais and took the ferry across to Dover. After another three-hour truck ride, we were ready to begin the tour.

Dually was a hit with the fans. For him, we created an oval arena, larger than I used for my other demonstrations. Half a dozen steers were released into the pen and I'd put him through his paces. I would identify the steer I wanted to cut out of the group and Dually would go about his business. Once separated from his buddies, the steer would naturally try to get back to join them. With no cues from me, Dually would make incredible dives and spins to keep the steer separated from the others. The audience, who'd never seen this kind of thing before, was amazed.

We added a humorous touch with one of the girls who worked for us on the tour. She'd go into the ring and start off with her back to the fence up at one end. Her job was simple, all she had to do was get to the other side, any way she could. Dually stopped her, every time.

Meanwhile, I was proud to see the lines of people after the demonstrations, asking to have their copies of the book signed. It brought such an amazing feeling of acceptance for someone who, until this late stage in life, had to keep quiet about his work.

The highlight of the tour was an invitation from the Queen. She was interested in seeing the presentation with Dually and asked me to conduct a private showing at Windsor Castle for her and Princess Margaret.

So Dually took me back to Windsor Castle, where this new life of mine had begun. I believe Dually is the first, last and only horse ever to work cattle in the riding hall at Windsor Castle. The Queen and Princess Margaret enjoyed watching Dually very much, and I will always remember standing with Her Majesty for a photograph with this wonderful gelding that gave me so much pleasure.

Dually died in 2001 of an incurable joint disease, which took him from me all too young. He's buried at Flag Is Up near Johnny Tivio, Night Mist and Julia's Doll.

NUEBE

To date, we've conducted 1,200 public demonstration events over a fourteen-year period and we've not had to cancel one, or even start late. There have been some close calls but never a failure. Snow in Las Vegas knocked our tent down and practically stopped us, and flight schedules have put others in jeopardy, but each time the show went on.

Every horse was improved, even if a few could be considered slightly improved only. The vast majority, however, were dramatically changed before the eyes of more than a million people in total. It is impossible to remember every horse brought to me, and just as impossible to forget some of them.

In May 2002, we were in Munich. It was one o'clock in the afternoon and we were examining the horses on offer. My rider of five years, Jason Davis, was putting the horses through the round pen to give the veterinarian a chance to watch them trot. I was sitting outside speaking with the owners in an effort to decide which horses would make the best educational demonstrations. I had four categories to fill: the untrained horse, the horse with incorrigible ground manners, the bucker and the horse that refused to load in the trailer.

Nuebe, a six-year-old black stallion, was led into the round pen and, as Jason began work, I greeted the two ladies, both in their forties, who owned the horse. Their clothes, their demeanour and their conversation spoke volumes about their experience in the horse world and they were, in fact, professional trainers of dressage horses. They told me that Nuebe could easily be a world-class competition horse except for his deep fear of umbrellas.

'What?' I queried. 'Did I hear you right? He's frightened of umbrellas?'

About a year previously, one of the owners had been riding Nuebe in a competition in the Munich area. Summer thunderstorms are common in that part of the world and, while Nuebe was performing, one of these downpours had moved in. A man standing next to the rail had popped open a spring-loaded umbrella, which had set off a chain of events that caused injury to both rider and horse. The storm was very heavy and everyone began to open umbrellas as Nuebe ran through the show grounds in a panic.

Subsequently, no one could get near him with an umbrella. No matter how hard they tried, they could not convince him to accept the sight of one of these 'horrible instruments'. I enquired if they had an umbrella with them that day, which they had but were keeping hidden under the chairs. I asked one of my assistants to take it out, but told him to be careful because I had no way of knowing how serious the situation was. We remained outside the round pen and opened the umbrella just a little. Nuebe went ballistic. It was as dramatic a response as I've ever witnessed. Nuebe would injure himself if we persisted, so we folded up the umbrella and put it back under the seats.

I politely thanked the owners, marked down Nuebe as not suitable for a public demonstration and moved on to look at the next horse.

After all the horses had completed their trip to the round pen, I was about to tell Jason which ones I wanted for the evening when he said, 'You can do him, you know.'

'I can do who?' I asked.

'The black horse. You can fix him.'

'Are you out of your mind?' I replied. 'I have a sold-out building with five thousand seats and you want me to do a horse like that? I've never dealt with an umbrella phobia in my life, and it seems to me to be incredibly risky. It would be inviting disaster.'

Jason looked at me with a wry smile and a twinkle in his eye. 'You can do him, Monty. It might be a great demonstration, and I'm convinced you'll cause him to accept the umbrella.'

Somewhere down inside of me I wanted to work with this horse, but without Jason's encouragement I never would have taken the chance. I agreed that we should accept Nuebe for the second phase of the evening's demonstration. It was dangerous, but we had to give it a try.

Working to overcome Nuebe's phobia in Munich, Germany, 2001

When Nuebe came into the ring the audience expressed a collective gasp at how beautiful he was. The house lights were off and the round pen was bathed in heavy stage lights. His coat shone like polished onyx. His carriage was regal during join-up and Nuebe soon seemed to find me a friendly partner in an otherwise strange world of lights and the sound of 5,000 people on the edge of their seats, curious to see what would happen next. Jason brought the umbrella into the pen and Nuebe put on a show that froze every spectator, even with the 'horrible instrument' fully closed. Meanwhile, I related over the sound system the story behind his strange phobia.

When the umbrella opened, Nuebe ran frantically, trying to get as far from it as he could. Sand flew through the air, reaching people well into the body of the audience. His eyes were like saucers, his head high and his nostrils flared wide open, blowing hot breath. The sound of his snorting must have put a chill in the people; it certainly did in me.

Directing Jason to close the umbrella, I began to walk around the round pen, wondering just what the heck I would do. I needed Nuebe to trust me and I worked hard on getting my adrenaline down and lowering my pulse rate. I schooled Nuebe on the Dually halter until he came to understand and respect it, and then began to work with an artificial arm I use, which I am sure to Nuebe resembled an umbrella. It was larger but did not open, and soon I could rub his body with it. I used the full complement of the language equus to tell Nuebe I intended him no harm, and I did my best to impart to him that I would protect him from all killer umbrellas; he was safe with me.

After about ten minutes, I had Jason bring me the umbrella, which I gathered close to the arm, and once more went through the same litany of discussion I had with the arm on its own. Within three or four minutes, Nuebe accepted the arm and the umbrella together. Next, I sent the arm out of the ring and continued my work with just the umbrella. Within a minute or so, I was massaging Nuebe's body with the thing he dreaded most in life. He was sweating and trembling but trying hard to believe in me. This was what join-up could achieve. Perhaps more than ever before, I felt that I was on the right track. Join-up is something that everyone should know about. It really could dramatically improve the relationship between man and horse.

I opened the large umbrella slightly and massaged Nuebe with the loose material on one side, and I promised him there'd be no pain associated with what he perceived to be a threat. Slowly, I opened it more and more, and Nuebe's trust in me gradually overcame his fear. I could hear my audience beginning to murmur to one another and I realized I was still surrounded by 5,000 people. I suddenly became aware that I hadn't heard a sound from them for the past fifteen minutes or so. With the umbrella wide open, I began to move it around Nuebe, and while he was obviously troubled, he didn't blast away.

Gradually I moved around the pen, opening and closing the umbrella and holding it high over my head. The lead line was attached to the Dually halter but he was following me without tugging on it.

It crossed my mind to say thank you very much ladies and gentlemen, end that segment of the evening and send Nuebe to the stable – but I decided to go further. In my mind I could see Jason's face and the twinkle in his eye. Somehow I knew that he wanted me to stretch myself to make the difference between a good demonstration and a great one.

I reached out, unsnapped the line from the halter and tossed it out of the way, towards the gate. Then I moved in a large circle with the umbrella fully open and raised over my head. Nuebe followed me, as if he was saying, yes, I can do it, I can overcome this phobia.

What happened next was a first for me, and it certainly hasn't happened since that time. The soundman turned the music up and the audience began to clap. Nuebe was frightened by the audience's response but I immediately noticed it only served to bring him closer to me. Walking faster, I realized that Nuebe had picked up his pace in order to stay closer to me – even though I had the 'horrible instrument' fully open. The audience somehow knew it was OK to applaud and Nuebe and I received a standing ovation that persisted for two to three minutes.

I thanked everyone and asked for silence so I could continue. I began to rub Nuebe between the eyes and around the head as a gesture of appreciation for the courage he'd shown. I walked once more around the ring, umbrella open and umbrella closed, in order to give Nuebe a chance to come down from what had been a very traumatic experience for him. I sensed his adrenaline levels dropping. The demonstration was over.

As Nuebe left the arena, the audience sprang to their feet and once more gave us a standing ovation. Many stomped the floor, whistled and called out in appreciation of what they had seen.

As a child, I had become frightened of the objects my father used to punish me – whips, ropes, even polo mallets were feared by me just as Nuebe feared the umbrella. He'd needed to find trust, affection and understanding. He needed to know that he was safe from violence and bodily harm. Join-up could give him that trust. I felt huge pride and, at the same time, humility at this incredible demonstration of the power of the language I call equus.

SHY BOY

This is a book about the horses in my life and so, although Shy Boy has a book of his own, *Shy Boy: The Horse That Came in From the Wild*, it's essential he's included.

Once I had gained some recognition from the general public for my work, I began to receive various requests from the media. One of these was an approach from the BBC in London, asking if I had any idea of how they might make a programme that would explain my concepts to a wider audience, not just horse people.

By now I had laid to rest the lack of acceptance from my father and others. After all, I could prove my theories were effective and had done so in front of thousands of people in countless towns and cities around the world, and my book was an international bestseller. If I wanted acceptance and approval of my ideas, I had more than anyone could wish for. Yet there was one thing from my past that I hadn't laid to rest. It was the time when I'd gone out into the wilderness, up in the high ranges of Nevada, and performed join-up in the wild with Buster. As described earlier, when I'd ridden Buster back to the ranch, the cowboys had suggested I must have found a mustang that had already been ridden. They just didn't believe what I'd done. It still rankled. I had been so full of pride and excitement that day and no one believed me.

I suggested to the BBC that I could try to do the same thing again, and the cameras would be there to see how I got on. I would try to perform join-up in the wild. The BBC loved the idea and set about making the arrangements.

Dr Robert Millar, veterinarian and renowned animal behaviourist, was hired to act as a referee of sorts. He would verify the legitimacy of the mustang and the procedures, and would ensure the horse was properly cared for, as well as being available for any medical needs that might arise. Laurence Scanlon, the editor of my first book, was to come along as an observer.

The first step was to adopt a wild mustang from the Bureau of Land Management, the federal agency that controls wild horses in the United States. I called him Shy Boy. I was careful to have no contact with him whatsoever, so that he remained completely wild.

So there we were, forty years on, up in the high desert, just me and this wild mustang with no ropes, no fences, nothing – oh, except a film crew. That gave it a different feel, for sure, but there was going to be no disputing what happened this time. Every inch of my work would be shown in living colour.

Shy Boy joined up with me in exactly twenty-four hours, as I had predicted to the BBC several months earlier in London. Here was this wild horse, choosing to be with me rather than to flee into the thousands of acres of wilderness that beckoned in every direction. I had a halter and surcingle (belly band) on him in thirty-six hours. Each step of the plan stayed within a few hours of the schedule. Within seventy-two hours, I had a rider on Shy Boy's back and he was cantering along following our saddle horses. Independent observers had verified every step. Join-up between man and horse worked, even in the wild.

The documentary was shown around the world over the next three years or so, and the fact is there are sceptics who still don't believe what I did to this day. Psychologists could describe the relationship forged between Shy Boy and me, as I followed him through the backcountry, as catastrophic bonding. I fell in love with the horse during that week to ten days.

Shy Boy went to a student of mine, Ron Ralls, for further training as a working cow horse while I travelled the world promoting *The Man Who Listens to Horses*. Shy Boy took his lessons well and became an even-tempered, cooperative equine student.

Journalists and readers often asked about Shy Boy. People wanted to know where he was and how he was doing. Many came up with the same question: 'What do you think Shy Boy would do if you took him back out to the wilderness and released him with the same herd of horses?' My answer had to be, 'I don't know.' I didn't believe anyone had done that before and so no one could have a good answer, but I was interested to find out and eleven months after the first adventure, we set out to film another documentary. The plan was to return to the place where the first one was filmed, release Shy Boy when we found his familiar herd, and see what his response would be. I was convinced that the horses would kick him out immediately. He had been on domestic feed and drinking water from a different area so his body would give off a totally different scent from that of the family group.

I was wrong. They took him back in like he'd been away for just a day or so. Not one of them said a negative word to him. It was about three o'clock in the afternoon when we released him and by dark he was miles from us with his group of horses. I told everyone in the group he would either come back in the night or first thing in the morning. I actually felt certain we would see him around our campsite at dawn.

I was wrong again. At daylight he was nowhere to be seen but at about nine o'clock the following morning he turned up on top of a hill about a quarter of a mile from our location. He stopped for a few seconds, looked back at the other horses and then cantered down off the hill and directly to me. It was one of the most moving experiences of my career.

Shy Boy was home to stay and has never been away from us since that moment. He lives on Flag Is Up Farms and I feel certain he believes he owns the place. Pat rides him as much as anyone does, and his regular job is to escort young horses to and from the riding arenas and training track on our farm. He shows young Thoroughbreds how to go through the starting gate and is quite capable of assisting young cutting horses or reined cow horses by helping with the duties of controlling the cattle they are working.

Shy Boy is one of the gentlest horses on the face of this earth. When the documentaries are being aired across the country, I often take him with me to the television studios. He walks over the cables and under the spotlights. Shy Boy loves children and they certainly love him. I often take him to events where children come to meet him and he seems to have a great time enjoying their company. We have a special blanket he wears with his name on it. It works in conjunction with a very effective diaper that he wears for obvious reasons. He also sports four rubber hoof jackets, which prevent him from slipping on floors made for people.

One time, on a demonstration tour of the north west, we took Shy Boy because five public television studios plus affiliates wanted him to be present for the airing of the documentaries. He had appearances in Medford, Oregon, Seattle, Yakima, Washington, Ogden, Utah and Denver. In Yakima, for a morning show, Jason Davis, my rider and assistant at the time, prepared Shy Boy and, at the agreed moment, led him in and presented him to the host, who was interviewing me. We were engaged in a great conversation when I heard a strange sound towards Shy Boy's rear legs. I couldn't look back to see what was going on but, suddenly, a familiar smell began to permeate the air of the studio. When we cut for a commercial, I turned to see Jason, red-faced, coming in with a shovel and a black plastic bag. He looked at me sheepishly and said that he had forgotten to zip up the bottom of Shy Boy's diaper. The staff of that television studio are probably still telling stories about Shy Boy's visit to their station.

In San Antonio, Texas, at a meeting of grammar school principals from all over the United States, I was a co-keynote speaker and Shy Boy was my

Shy Boy racing the wind in 1998

sidekick. There were 6,000 people in one room in a huge convention centre and no opportunity for a rehearsal. We just had to get on with it. Shy Boy and I proceeded down the centre aisle towards a very large stage, which fortunately had a wheelchair ramp at one end. The mustang walked up the ramp, right out to the centre of the stage, where he stood, ears up, viewing his audience. Shy Boy had no idea why he received a standing ovation but he was totally calm while 6,000 people produced deafening applause.

At the conclusion of our presentation, Shy Boy walked back down the ramp and stood quietly while literally thousands of people came to say hello to him. I've known a lot of horses in my time but I don't believe I've ever seen one that could have tolerated this environment with the tranquillity exhibited by Shy Boy.

The most recent important event in Shy Boy's life involved the Rose Bowl Parade on 1 January 2003. The officials of this enormous event asked me to take part to represent the work I do with horses. The Rose Bowl Parade is a New Year's Day tradition in Pasadena, California, where it has taken place for over a hundred years and is regarded as the warm-up to the grandfather of all college football games, the Rose Bowl.

The parade begins at about 8.30 a.m. and follows a five-mile route down Colorado Boulevard. Approximately one million people are on site to view it in person. The air force does low fly-overs with stealth bombers and a large portion of the parade is made up of huge floats with enormous moving parts. Each float has its own music emanating from somewhere inside and the city is filled with a mixture of utterly unique sounds. Marching bands and baton-twirling beauties compete for rousing applause as the parade moves along at about two and a half miles per hour.

The parade officials were interested in paying tribute to the American mustang and I had the most famous American mustang in the world. I was excited about the prospect of being a part of this massive extravaganza and had complete confidence that Shy Boy could handle the incredible challenge the parade would present. It then transpired that they wanted six mustangs to be involved, some to come from Indian reservations as opposed to being all from the Bureau of Land Management. This meant we needed to train five mustangs – and we had five months to get the job done.

Shy Boy proved extremely helpful in the process of educating five other recently captured horses that were as wild as deer. Jason was the primary trainer because I was on the road virtually the whole time the preparation of these horses was taking place. I can claim very little credit for getting them ready to face one of the most daunting environments any horse has ever met.

At 14.1 hands and 950 pounds, Shy Boy is on the small side to look appropriate under me although I have ridden him many times, and with that in mind, we decided Pat should ride Shy Boy in the parade. Linda Klausner was the equine coordinator for the parade and she filled us in on what we might expect on 1 January. Linda told us we would follow a float that went by the name of 'The Candy Man'. Huge and festively decorated, it was designed to attract the attention of the children and, in fact, children seemed to be leaning from every part of it, throwing candy to the masses of people as we moved along. The float that followed us was complete with a dragon about twenty feet tall. He would roar every twenty seconds or so and blow huge amounts of steam from his nostrils, each of which was about two feet in diameter.

Linda told us a favourite pastime of youngsters at the side of the parade was to throw firecrackers under the horses passing by. Confetti and tickertape would be thrown from the buildings and horses were often spooked by the jet aircraft flying low.

We had to be in the staging area by ten o'clock the evening before the parade and we got very little sleep, saddling up around 4.30 a.m. and making sure our tack and costumes were in order for a 6.30 departure. We rode to the start, about two miles away. The horses performed admirably with Shy Boy showing them the way. I rode Navajo, a mustang that stands nearly 16.0 hands and weighs about 1,200 pounds. While he was not as comfortable with his surroundings as Shy Boy, he behaved in a very acceptable fashion.

All six horses completed the five miles without a single negative step. Shy Boy seemed to know he had done a good job when we arrived at the schoolyard at the end of Colorado Boulevard, which was designated as the finishing point for the equestrian participants. I was so proud of them all.

Shy Boy has his own box stall for sleeping and a field for daily turnouts. He is visited by literally hundreds of people each week, who ask to see him when they stop by the farm. He has a home here for the rest of his life, and my relationship with him is as close as I've had with any horse. Shy Boy is a wonderful little American mustang and a great tribute to those survivors of the early Spanish settlers in the western part of the United States.

JOHNNY TIVIO

I have left the most important horse in my life until last – Johnny Tivio. To tell his story takes me back to when I was younger and stronger than I am now. At the age of sixty-nine, with five vertebrae welded together, I often think how wonderful it was that Johnny Tivio and I enjoyed the prime of life together.

Johnny Tivio was a blood bay Quarter Horse stallion born on 24 April 1956. He was the result of mating Poco Tivio with a Green Cattle Company mare wearing the R O brand. She was small and was raised near the California town of Chowchilla. I suppose that's how she came by the name Chowchilla Peewee. In the early days of the state of California, the Green Cattle Company was an enormous ranching operation that spread from northern California all the way down into Mexico. Their registered brand was R O. Charles Araujo of Coalinga, California, acquired Chowchilla Peewee in the 1940s. I don't suppose anybody knew her actual breeding. Her registration papers came into existence when an inspection process allowed horses to be registered as Quarter Horses. Apparently Chowchilla Peewee met the criteria and so she received a number.

Charles Araujo sold Johnny Tivio as a yearling to a man from Bakersfield, California, by the name of Carl Williams. Mr Williams was not a professional horseman but he had property near trainer Bob Mettler, who started Johnny Tivio at two years of age. When a different trainer moved into the neighbourhood, Carl Williams, for one reason or another, sent Johnny Tivio to him.

The second trainer, who shall remain nameless, decided to enter Johnny Tivio in competition, starting early in his third year, and not just in one but in two separate disciplines, the hackamore and the cutting. Johnny won no championships in those early days but no one could expect that. The fact is, though, that Johnny Tivio caught the eye of every professional who watched him work.

While not beautifully conformed, Johnny had one of the most gorgeous coats seen anywhere. He had an outstanding head and neck, and while his body conformation was less than Rembrandt might have chosen to paint, he moved like the consummate athlete he turned out to be.

This second trainer was not one to be too serious about his responsibilities, and most of the professionals I travelled with thought his treatment of Johnny was less than he deserved.

Johnny Tivio's age put him square in line to compete with my prospect Fiddle D'Or in 1960. I planned my year of competition and worked hard to give Fiddle every opportunity to maximize his efforts. Johnny Tivio was not given the same consideration. Pat would often say to me, 'Man, you're lucky Johnny Tivio is being trained by this particular fellow. I don't think Fiddle could ever beat him if a responsible trainer was in charge.'

In midsummer, Pat and I were on the circuit and, as I recall, I was showing My Blue Heaven in the open working cow horse class and Fiddle D'Or in the hackamore. We arrived one night in Watsonville, California. Just outside the town, on the road to the fairgrounds, we drove by a honky-tonk saloon and Pat pointed to it.

'Look at that truck over there,' she said. 'That's the guy who's showing Johnny Tivio.'

The truck was full of horses. It was the type of vehicle used to haul cattle and often referred to as slat-sided so you could see the animals through the walls.

We went on to the fairgrounds, unloaded our horses, watered them and gave them twenty minutes of walking and trotting as they had just completed a five-hour journey. We housed them in their assigned stalls with a comfortable bed and food and water. Unhooking the trailer, we headed back to town to check in at our hotel. I believe it was around 9.30 p.m. when we passed the saloon for the second time. The truck was still there and the horses were still inside.

We were up again at about five as the preliminary competition was to begin around eight o'clock. On the fairgrounds, we cleaned, fed and watered our horses, giving them a chance to collect themselves before we began to tack up. Pat went to the horse-show office to do the normal bookwork and pick up our numbers. Walking back to our stable, she noticed that the stalls allocated to Johnny Tivio's trainer were still empty.

I believe it was around 7.00 a.m. when we began to saddle up and as long as I live I will never forget what we saw in the next half hour. The stables were at the bottom of a hill and the approach road was quite steep. We watched as the truck we recognized from the saloon came roaring down the hill. It came to a stop near the arena and the trainer got out on the driver's side. A rather dishevelled looking woman got out on the passenger side.

Pure reining: Johnny and me on our way to victory

The trainer lowered the ramp and I recognized each of the horses he unloaded and tied to the side of the truck, including Johnny Tivio. He threw the saddles on immediately and then led them one by one to a large communal water trough, allowing them to drink their fill. As you may imagine, each took a large quantity of water as they had just spent the night without a sip. The trainer tied them back to the side of the truck with the exception of Johnny Tivio. He put a hackamore on Johnny and climbed into the saddle. Then he grabbed the woman by the arm and swung her up just behind his saddle. 'Hang on,' he said and into the arena they went at a full canter, her arms wrapped around his middle like a passenger on a motorcycle. For the next ten minutes or so he navigated the arena, introducing his new friend to other trainers, cantering, stopping and spinning Johnny Tivio, so as to make it a thrilling ride for her.

I remarked to Pat that there was no way Johnny Tivio could beat us today and how sad it was, but Fiddle D'Or was definitely getting an unfair advantage over a superior opponent who had no chance in this competition. We competed in the preliminaries and both horses made it to the finals. Fiddle D'Or finished second and Johnny Tivio won the class. Fiddle didn't finish second very many times. The fact that I won the world championship with Fiddle D'Or that season was not because he was the world's best – it was because the world's best was not given the opportunity to prove himself.

After the Watsonville incident, I said to Pat, 'I want to own that horse some day. The world should know just how good he really is.'

They didn't campaign Johnny Tivio in the hackamore in 1961, and the field was left to Fiddle without his toughest competition. Johnny was shown sparingly and mostly in the cutting. Irresponsibility was costing this trainer and we got word that Carl Williams was taking Johnny home for extended periods of time. Throughout the 1961 and 1962 seasons, I saw Carl Williams on several occasions and each time I mentioned that if Johnny was ever for sale, I was seriously interested. In the autumn of 1962, the situation came to a head in King City, California.

A citizen reported that a truck had been parked for two days with animals inside. There didn't appear to be any food or water available and the animals needed urgent care. The authorities broke in. When they checked, they found that the truck was registered to Carl Williams and they went to his house with the intention of charging him with animal cruelty, only to find the truck had been in the hands of the trainer. While there were other horses aboard, Johnny Tivio was the only one that belonged to Carl Williams.

Mr Williams remembered our earlier conversations and called me to let me know the time had come for a parting of the ways with this trainer. He wanted to sell Johnny Tivio. I immediately went over and made the transaction. George A. Smith, a client of mine, and I bought him in partnership and I held the option to buy out Mr Smith. The price was $6,000, and to me that seemed an absolute steal. However, Carl Williams told me that because of all of the neglect, Johnny Tivio had suffered acute laminitis and the vets would not give him a clean report as a competition horse, although they thought he could function normally for breeding.

When I arrived at the stable, I was shocked to see Johnny's condition. He was 150 pounds underweight and his front feet were low in the heel and elongated by about 30 per cent. From the X-rays, though, the skeletal changes seemed minimal. Johnny's coat that had been like burnished bronze was dull with none of its previous brilliance. We bought the horse holding out great hopes that, with proper foot care and nutrition, we could get him back in the show ring.

I took my time getting acquainted with Johnny, allowing him to tell me when he was ready for physical activity. My farrier, J.R. Jennings, did a remarkable job getting those front feet back in working order. Each evening I found myself discussing with Pat how excited I was about this new member of our family. I thought he had more natural ability than any horse I had ever seen.

By the spring of 1964, Johnny Tivio had the lustre back in his coat, a spring in his step and a new pair of front feet with which to dance through his routines as no horse before him ever could. I knew his performances by heart from the previous three years, and what I saw coming from him now was another dimension of excellence, far above the level of performance at Watsonville or any of the other places.

The day came for the entries to close for the 1964 Salinas competition. Other than the Grand National finals, Salinas was the granddaddy event for working cow horses. Before entering Salinas, I remember calling Pat to the arena one day, saying, 'Watch Johnny and tell me whether I should enter him in the cutting or the reined cow horse class. Which is his strongest event?' Pat watched him and I believe her level of amazement equalled mine.

'Why don't you enter him in both?' she asked.

Johnny and me winning a cutting championship

'You can't do that! It's probably against the rules, but you just couldn't do it anyway.'

I thought, along with most other Western trainers, that it was virtually impossible to ask a horse to mix the disciplines of cutting and reined cow work. Cutting asks the horse to stay back away from his cattle, keeping them from returning to the herd, while the reined cow horse is asked to go forward and control the animal. The two contradict one another to such an extent that I know of no one who ever held the opinion that they could be executed within the same time frame. Someone once told me that to ask a reined cow horse to compete in the cutting was a little like asking a foxhound to gather the sheep.

Pat reminded me that she did most of the rule reading and she couldn't remember anything against competing in both events at Salinas. We headed straight for the house, grabbed the little Salinas rulebook and began poring over it. It wasn't there! Nowhere **did it say this** was not allowed. Pat filled out the form, entering Johnny in the 1964 Salinas competition in both the cutting and the working cow horse events.

Four or five days later, Pat called to me in the stable and said that Lester Sterling was on the phone. Lester Sterling was a name from my past. He had been the chairman of the Salinas event for many years, and I was raised on the competition grounds where this contest was held. Lester Sterling was the decision maker and I knew this phone call wasn't going to be a comfortable one.

After I said hello, he shouted down the phone, 'Have you gone mad? Monty, I've known you since you were born. I know you're not stupid, and I don't want you to embarrass yourself or our show. No horse can perform in both the cutting and the reined cow horse competition in the same week. It's just not possible!' He went on to say he had read the rules and, while they didn't preclude this entry, he just didn't feel he could let it happen.

I reminded him that the public did not view the preliminary competitions and, if the horses weren't good enough to go forward into the later levels of the tournament-style event, the paying audience would not have the opportunity to watch their performance. That would keep any embarrassment down to competitors and committee people. I told him I had my hands on a horse that wasn't about to embarrass anybody, and that if there was any embarrassment, it should be in the way Johnny was shown in the past and not in the way he would perform now.

Lester Sterling allowed the entry and Johnny responded by performing in front of two entirely separate sets of judges and under totally different environmental circumstances. Sitting on his back, I thought to myself that I was in the presence of greatness. I didn't show him; he showed me, and the rest of the world, too, that this business of being a working cow horse and a cutting horse in the same week was no problem, at least, not for him. Johnny won both competitions and he did it in a way that left no question about who the winner was. A large margin of points separated first and second in both contests.

They changed the rules straight afterwards. No horse has ever been allowed to repeat this double competition. I suppose that's a little like retiring the number of a Hall of Fame athlete. It seems fitting that Johnny Tivio is not only the first horse ever to accomplish this incredible feat, but it's likely he'll be the only one.

Johnny Tivio went on to win four world championships and, in 1976, was one of the first horses to be inducted into the National Reined Cow Horse Association Hall of Fame. His trophies are hanging on our walls but I sometimes think, fancifully, if the positions were reversed, there should be somewhere for Johnny to hang me up. He could show all the horses of the world how he was able to train a young horseman to perform at true world-class level.

I competed on Johnny Tivio in virtually every event where the horse carries a Western saddle and he was world class in virtually all of these disciplines. Dean Oliver, arguably the greatest calf roper who ever lived, roped on Johnny several times and was amazed at his level of skill, even though it was far from his speciality. I could go on relating stories about him until this book and two more were full but just two exemplify how overwhelming was his talent.

His unusual ability to perform in such a wide variety of contests led me, in 1964, to shoot for those championships they call All-Around. At one class-A Quarter Horse Show, I entered him for everything in sight, including the Western riding, which is a form of Western dressage. Western riding was a newcomer to the world of Quarter Horse shows at that time, and while the elements of the discipline were present in the routines that preceded it, neither Johnny nor I had any experience with this contest as such. I had never trained him in Western riding and I had never shown a horse in that particular event before. It involved flying lead changes, controlled walk, trot and canter, stopping, turning and backing up in some very precise ways.

Johnny and I were in the main arena, competing in the cutting, when there was an announcement that I was due in an outside ring to perform in the Western riding. If I was to compete at all, they had to wait for me, as my events were conducted simultaneously. Pat was keeping a running record of where I stood in the race for the All-Around, or High-Point, Championship. She came to the side of the ring to tell me that if I did well in the cutting and placed in the Western riding, I would win the All-Around Championship but it might be close. Hobby Horse, a four-year-old, was winning everything in the junior division, which was restricted to horses of four years and younger. Hobby Horse, ridden by Red Neil, a friend of mine, had weak competition in his events.

I can't remember exactly where we finished in the cutting, either second or third. Pat met me at the out gate with the headgear necessary for the Western riding competition. We quickly changed the bridle and I trotted off to ring number two where forty or fifty contestants were sitting around in various stages of agitation. They had finished competing nearly half an hour ago and had to wait for me to go through the course.

Clyde Kennedy was the judge. He was world class and, as a trainer, had been responsible for many champions in both the Western and the hunter/jumper division. Mr Kennedy was a superstar horseman, who had been a qualified judge with the American Horse Shows Association for probably twenty years at the time of this contest.

As if it was yesterday, I can remember riding into the ring. What happened in the next four minutes or so will never fade from my memory, nor will it fade from the memories of the other impatient competitors. I was a passenger on the greatest performance horse in the world. Clyde Kennedy marked him with the highest score he had ever given; it also turned out to be the co-highest score Johnny Tivio ever received. I was blown away, and so were some of the professional Western-riding specialists, who simply could not believe it was Johnny's first trip through the course.

I went on to show Johnny in twelve more Western riding competitions over the next two years and, to this day, his record in that event remains unbeaten. Johnny Tivio added another Register of Merit to his long list of awards thanks to the Western riding that we would not even have entered if it hadn't been for our desire to win the High-Point Championship.

With the creation of Flag Is Up Farms on the horizon, 1966 would be the last full year of competition for Johnny. It was a long and hard year for him; the competition was getting tougher all the time, and the shows more numerous. I had set a goal – to win the cutting championship for the seven western states. We reduced the number of non-cutting competitions that we entered, and went all out to achieve what virtually no horse had ever done before, which was to win this cutting championship as well as the reined cow horse championships he already had to his credit.

Johnny Tivio was the 1966 Champion Cutting Horse for the Pacific Coast Cutting Horse Association, which included the seven western states. With that championship in hand, I set a new goal for us and that was to go to the American Quarter Horse Association finals at the Cow Palace and to close Johnny's career by winning the High-Point Championship. This meant that we had to refocus our attention on a wide array of disciplines if we were going to compete once more in the various events and win at his last show.

George A. Smith was still a 50 per cent partner in Johnny, and he and his wife Kathy had a lot of fun being involved in the career of this incredible individual. They came to the Cow Palace full of hope and support, but also mindful of the challenges Johnny and I faced. We started slowly and at the mid-way point I had come first in just one competition and that was the calf roping. I think I was about fourth in the cutting and third in the working cow horse. Don Dodge was sailing on a horse called Right Now and had three victories in the bag.

We were down to two contests, the open Western riding and the all-age reining. Johnny Tivio was never beaten in Western riding, so I was able to get one more first place under my belt before going to the final class, which was the reining championship.

Johnny T was never beaten in Western riding – he was the greatest!

The way the points were figured, the more horses that were in the class, the more points you got. As I recall, there were sixty-three performers in the pure reining. Johnny was a reined cow horse, and not a specialist in pure reining. The best reiners in the United States were there and it appeared our chances were extremely slim. Arithmetically, I could win the High Point, but only if I was first in that final reining competition. The Smiths came and said they felt they had better get on the road. They had meetings in Sacramento and they gave us big hugs, suggesting that while Johnny gave his best, there was just no possibility of winning the High-Point Championship.

Right back to the time of Brownie, I had a routine that I reserved for those moments in my career I felt were super important. I would ride my horse well away from everybody else and we would go through some exercises designed, I suppose, more for me than for my horse. These sessions had to be rare so that I was not constantly asking myself, or my horse, for supernatural performance. Johnny Tivio understood this routine better than any other horse I have known. He seemed to comprehend the importance of the moment. It may have seemed a waste of time to most professional trainers but I often felt that these quiet moments placed our brainwaves in step with one another.

If ever there was a need for this theory to work, it was then. I rode Johnny to a part of the Cow Palace complex that I will never forget. We had our time together and I felt we were prepared. I remember riding back towards the main arena with a renewed feeling of confidence. I could feel a quickening of Johnny's steps and an elevated resolve within him. As it came closer to our time to perform, I could run a video in my head of what we needed to do to win. I could see Johnny accomplishing an incredible routine, and there was a smile on my face as I rode into the arena.

With the championship in mind, a second-place finish would be no better than sixty-third and so we went all out. Our performance was virtually flawless and I believe that my smile just got larger throughout the routine. Johnny Tivio won first place, a saddle and a silver and gold belt buckle, presented to me by a man named Wes Eade. As he handed us our trophies, he said that he'd just seen the impossible.

You can imagine my telephone conversation that evening with George Smith. George was close to eighty years of age and he was extremely happy with the unbelievable result. George said that Pat and I should be the sole owners of Johnny Tivio in retirement and we could pay him back from stallion fees. This was done within a year and Johnny belonged to us completely.

So Johnny, a Quarter Horse, stood at stud on a major Thoroughbred operation and, while Thoroughbred people would think him inferior to their wonderful racehorses, Johnny was fully of the opinion that Flag Is Up was his property and that he was in charge of the activities there. We were able to give him his own field during the day and a wonderful stable for the nighttime. He had his harem and at just ten years of age he could look forward to many years of contentment.

I rode Johnny often for the next seven or eight years and, while we worked cattle and surveyed the farm with regularity, there was never again the need to perform with the kind of intensity reserved for competition. Champion Thoroughbred jockeys Bill Shoemaker and Laffit Pincay rode Johnny during his retirement and never forgot their experience. Pat would often ride Johnny while instructing our three children in the skills of horsemanship.

People often ask me if I think horses enjoy being ridden. I usually answer by saying that it depends on how the riding is done and who the rider is. I tell them about Johnny and about how certain I am that he enjoyed every minute of being ridden. You don't have to be a genius to see when a horse is having fun and Johnny would tell you clearly that it was fun. He made many trips to other ranches with Pat and me to gather cattle or ride through the mountains just for the heck of it.

Johnny helped me in a profound manner with every horse that followed him, and I could fill a hundred pages with the details of those lessons. The most important thing I learned from Johnny, however, was that when he was abused and forced, he didn't reach his full potential. When the environment was changed so there was request rather than demand, when there was love instead of neglect, he was able to perform like no other horse before him. Johnny Tivio is not just burned into my memory, but he has made an indelible mark on hundreds of Western trainers and certainly on the industry in which he performed.

My last hours with Johnny were, as you may imagine, some of the most bittersweet of my life. We all have to die and that time will come for each of us, horse and human alike. The lifespan of horses dictates that most of us will outlive our equine partners.

I was at Hollywood Park racetrack early one morning in April 1981, watching the racehorses train, and left for home at approximately 10.00 a.m. I arrived back at Flag Is Up sometime around one, drove directly to the farm office and met Pat as I came through the door. Immediately, I realized that something was very wrong. Pat embraced me.

'Johnny Tivio,' she said through tears, 'is dead.'

Johnny had been in his pasture and observing a mare being led past his field on her way to the breeding barn. He had stepped up on his toes, lifted his tail and was trotting along the roadway parallel with the mare when, all of a sudden, the men saw him drop like a stone. Dr Van Snow, our resident veterinarian at that time, confirmed that he'd suffered a massive heart attack. Through my sadness, I was relieved that he had not suffered. In fact, I could say that he died smiling, thinking about the mare.

Johnny had been left where he'd fallen. As Pat and I walked towards his body, I could see the lifeless eyes. After a few minutes, Pat gave me a hug and walked away, realizing that I needed to spend time alone with Johnny. All the strength I'd felt from being relieved that he hadn't suffered deserted me. I stayed there with Johnny Tivio, replaying in my mind the good times we'd had together. I tried to overcome my sorrow with the knowledge I had been the luckiest person in the world to spend so many years with this old friend. We'd had a long time together. In recent years, Johnny had enjoyed the good life with a warm box stall at night and his beloved grass paddock during the day. From this paddock he could watch everything going on at the farm. Mares moving to and from the breeding barn had to pass him and every time they did, Johnny became the big stallion again, calling out and travelling the length of his field like a three-year-old.

I walked around him in the field, rerunning episodes from our life together. I re-enacted contests won and lost and talked to him about times funny and sad. I felt like a child, and it seemed that somehow revisiting these memories of our time together would keep his life from leaving. His life has never left me, and I, as well as those around me, will be forever affected by the time that he was with us. I remember kneeling behind him and lying over his shoulders.

Retired on Flag Is Up Farms in 1968

As he lay collapsed on his side, with that heavy, final weight that only death brings, I knew where to bury him. For some time, I'd had it in my mind to make a special graveyard just in front of the farm office, where I would give each horse his own headstone. Johnny Tivio would be the first. I would put the horses' names, dates and a line or two about their qualities or personalities on an engraved bronze plaque set into blocks of stone.

I dug his grave myself, using the farm's backhoe. By then it was dark, but the hole was dug and Johnny Tivio's body had to be lowered into it. This was the toughest part. I knew I would never again have a friend like Johnny and I could not bring myself to cover him with earth; I couldn't do it. Dr Snow volunteered to carry on while I went up to the house and crawled underneath the covers.

A few days later, when Pat was sending Johnny's American Quarter Horse registration papers to the Association to inform them of his death, she made an amazing discovery. Johnny had died on his twenty-fifth birthday. The plaque on his gravestone reads: 'Johnny Tivio, April 24, 1956 to April 24, 1981. Known to all as the greatest all-around working horse ever to enter an arena.'

Johnny Tivio seemed to have it in his mind to please me in whatever way he could. I think he believed he was the only horse in my life. Johnny never knew there would be a Lomitas, Shy Boy or Dually. No horse can speak in the language of humans, but I believe that if Johnny could have talked to me at the time of his death, he would have told me to get busy. I think he would have made it clear his life was over; he was out of here, but I should go forward with those things I was able to learn while he was with me. It is my belief that Johnny would have reminded me how dedicated he was to being the best he could be. It's clear that he would have admonished me to take on that same state of mind for myself. He might have told me to stop mourning him and to get moving on making things better for horses and for people using the techniques he worked so hard to teach me. The fact is thousands of horses and people have benefited from the lessons Johnny helped me learn.

From where he is now, I hope that Johnny Tivio knows about this book. I hope he knows I met the Queen of England and that I've toured the world demonstrating the techniques I've discovered during a long life of horsemanship. I hope he knows he's the last horse in this book because isn't it always true that you should save the best for last and, Johnny Tivio, you were the best – you were GREAT!

CONCLUSION

When I look back, I can see how horse after horse carried me away from cruelty and towards kindness and understanding. The lessons I learned from the horses in my life form the basis of all my work and of the message I want to pass on to the world.

I was still a young boy when I first encountered the no-name mustang, who taught me the language equus. Without words, he told me it was unnecessary to treat horses harshly or cruelly, or to use the methods of my father and his forefathers, which are still widely employed today. It isn't necessary to break a horse's spirit, to dominate or subdue him. On the contrary, such techniques can be proved to be massively counter-productive. That realization led me to a lifetime's effort to improve the relationship between man and horse.

I've spent decades working towards banning whips in racing. While there has been a dramatic reduction in their use, there is strong resistance to banning them completely. Hey Sam, Prince of Darkness, Stanley and many others have encouraged me, through their memory, to continue with this effort. The Dually™ halter and the Monty Roberts starting-stalls blanket are products of lessons taught me by these tolerant individuals. I owe the wonderful horses of the world my undying efforts to create a better environment for them.

Since 1996, when my first book was launched, I have been fortunate to receive many awards, including, on 29 January 1998, the Founder's Award as Man of the Year from the American Society for the Prevention of Cruelty to

Animals. The awards have various titles but each of them is connected in some way to the horses in my life. I am the recipient of these gifts but the credit belongs to the horses.

My books and videos have provided me with the opportunity to deal with misunderstood and mistreated horses on a global basis. While most people want to be fair with our equine partners, often the actions of the misinformed create a horse's psychological problems. It appears that I have accepted the role of spokesman for the horse, bringing to the world methods that replace violence with communication and understanding.

As I write this, I am preparing for a trip to Sydney, Australia, where the use of whips behind the starting stalls has recently been banned. I am excited about presenting options to the racing fraternity of that country. Perhaps Australia can be a model for many countries to take up the same cause.

It is my dream to live long enough to see the majority of horsemen working in partnerships rather than slave/master relationships. I long for the day when the horse and human connection can be experienced so as to leave the horse with its dignity. Each individual I have included in this book has led me to yearn for a time when horsemen find joy in watching the generosity of horses with the freedom of choice. Relationships such as I have had with horses will lead to green pastures in retirement instead of cold-hearted destruction at the end of their careers.

Perhaps most importantly, I developed from my understanding of the language of equus the technique I called Join-Up®. Mustangs in the wild taught me how to emulate their gestures so I could let them know they could trust me. The results were startling but even I underestimated the power of join-up. The mustang mare not only trusted me, but also protected me from perceived danger as if I was her infant. The irony is that while I can communicate with horses, humans tend to disbelieve what they see. You might think it would be easier to communicate with people but, in fact, egos and traditions often get in the way.

The horses told me I was right – boy, did they tell me! The lessons those mustangs taught me early on in life carried me forward into a successful career, not only in rodeo and Western disciplines, but also in the Thoroughbred racing industry to a level I would never have believed. An Act, Alleged and Lomitas – these are just a few of the horses that are burned into my memory. The mustangs, however, were closer to nature than the élite individuals, and it was because of their lessons that I was allowed to succeed in world-class competition in a very gratifying way.

Julia's Doll taught me the need to keep an open mind and let the horse show you where its talent lies. The lessons of Rough Frolic were to show me that the most effective trainer is the one who stays out of the way of a good horse. Observe him in action, respect his choices and he will eventually be a champion. My Blue Heaven and Johnny Tivio were crystal clear in their efforts to show me that the great trainer does not make the horse perform – he causes the horse to want to.

Her Majesty, the Queen of England changed everything. She validated join-up and sent me on a tour of the UK and Ireland – and suddenly people started to believe what was happening before their eyes. Since the day I saw the Queen Mother with tears streaming down her face at the sight of her filly being started by my methods, I've been on a non-stop mission to demonstrate join-up to as many people as possible around the world. I am in the process of training instructors in every quarter of the globe to take my message forward. Soon, another generation will be doing the work better than I ever could.

This book has been a pleasure to write. I have re-lived dramas and crises, intense emotions, valleys and certainly peaks. I feel a deep humility about the experiences the horses in my life have given me, and it is my fervent hope that I can pass on these experiences to generations to come.

GLOSSARY

Blinkers A hood-like arrangement that restricts the vision of the horse.

Bulldogging Also known as steer wrestling. A rodeo competition in which the primary cowboy stops a steer by leaping from his horse and wrestling it to the ground.

Championship Won by scoring the highest number of points over a prolonged period of time against competition from several divisions or disciplines.

Cutting The sorting of cattle. It generally refers to separating one animal at a time from the herd while on horseback.

Disunited The horse's legs are used in the wrong sequence while cantering – the leading leg in front is opposite to the leading leg behind.

Dually™ halter The trademarked name of a particular halter invented by the author. With the use of the Dually™, numerous problems with horses can be addressed and fixed without pain or violence. The halter allows the handler to school an initially uncooperative horse. When the horse resists the Dually, it becomes smaller and less comfortable, and when he cooperates, the Dually gives immediate reward by expanding and becoming quite comfortable. Through its use, the handler can communicate with the horse, and willingness and relaxation will be achieved. Recently, an invention called a Gentle Leader has emerged on the scene to assist in the training and handling of man's best friend, the dog. A Gentle Leader acts upon a set of principles similar to the Dually.

Dummy or mannequin An imitation human form used to simulate a rider, for example stuffed clothing.

Finals A tournament-style competition for which those who have successfully competed in preliminary contests are eligible.

Flying changes, lead changes A change of leading leg while remaining at the canter, performed when all four legs are off the ground. The front and hind legs must change at the same time. Horses that cannot achieve a smooth flying change tend to be disunited and are less athletic in their work. It is a requirement of coordinated movement to travel on the right lead while making a turn to the right, and the left lead for a turn to the left.

Grand champion A title given to an individual achieving a level comparable to best in show. The title is granted to the best of all age groups or a collection of divisions within any given discipline.

Hackamore A bitless bridle, requiring a high degree of responsiveness from the horse.

Haze horse The mount of the hazer – the secondary cowboy – in bulldogging. The role of the haze horse is to keep the steer moving in a straight line.

In hand Leading rather than riding a horse. Competitions that are based on conformation, style and turnout are conducted in hand. The horse is shown with just a halter and no other tack.

Lead or leading leg The front leg with which the horse leads while cantering. The horse may have to change the leading leg (flying change) when moving round to the left or right. Horses moving in a left arc will travel more comfortably with the left legs reaching double the distance of the right legs. The opposite is true if the horse is negotiating a right arc.

Piaffe-like movement Best described as prancing in place – actually, a trot without forward movement.

Quarter Horse One of a breed of strong saddle horses developed in the western United States and originally trained for quarter-mile races.

Superior mudder A horse that performs best when the surface is muddy or deep.

Western riding competition A group of contests for horses ridden in a Western saddle, such as cutting, reining, working cow horse, pleasure and trail.

Western style riding A method of riding originated in the USA, using a Western saddle. This is constructed with more support for the rider, both front and rear, than the English saddle. Typically, it has a prominent pommel, which can be used to attach a rope for the purpose of controlling cattle or other horses. The common name of this feature is the horn. Apart from these characteristics, the Western saddle and the English saddle are quite similar, and I believe far too much is made of their differences. The disciplines in which the Western style of riding is used are cutting horse competitions, reined cow horse classes (which by definition include reining, working cattle from the herd or down the fence), reining (classes without the cattle phases), pleasure and trail. The Western style saddle is also used in most of the rodeo competitions, such as bulldogging, calf roping, team roping and barrel racing.

ACKNOWLEDGEMENTS

This is the fifth book that my wife, Pat, and I have worked on together. Amazingly, we discovered that Pat knew every one of the horses in my life with one exception, my first horse, Ginger. I thank Pat from the bottom of my heart for throwing her enthusiasm and endless hours into helping me put the stories together. She was my sounding board, my typist and my editor. She gathered photos from all over the world and from our archives so readers could have visuals of those special horses. Without Pat, it would have been impossible for me to complete *The Horses in My Life* given the many days I am away from home. When necessary, she even travelled with me, computer in hand, and together we made it happen.

Three people were willing to read the manuscript while it was still a 'work in progress'. Michael Schwartz, Sally King and Lee Rosenberg deserve special thanks, as they were the ones who volunteered for the first read and were responsible for exceptionally good input. To my English tour team, the instructors and students from the Monty Roberts International Learning Center, I send my thanks for your helpful suggestions.

Jane Turnbull, my English literary agent, has worked tirelessly to make sure we found the right publishers to obtain the largest readership from my first book onwards. Thanks, Jane, for being a staunch believer and for your pursuit of the perfect publishing company who not only believe in my concepts, but also believe in me. Thank you everyone at Headline for your enthusiasm and for helping make it easy to work with you throughout the editing and fine-tuning of my manuscript. I appreciate your confidence and help, especially my editor, Val Hudson, and Lorraine Jerram. You're a great team!

I want to acknowledge the rest of my family who help keep 'the balls in the air': daughter, Debbie, and son-in-law, Tom Loucks. I know I don't say thank you enough for what you do, so I'm publicly saying 'thank you' now. You help Pat and me make it happen. Thank you, daughter Laurel, for always caring and for your unconditional love.

PICTURE CREDITS
We would like to thank the following
for kindly supplying photographs for use in the book:

T. Abahzy: 95, 101, 126, 131; Si Almond: 18; R.A. Anderson: 56; George Axt: 1, 63, 222; Bancroft Photography: 193; APRH P. Bertrand et fils: 143; Click: 44-5; Christopher Dydyk: 217; June Fallow: 51, 60, 67, 74, 81, 225, 229, 233; Gestut Fahrhof: 185, 187 (top and bottom right), 188; Helene Glassman: 4, 5; Jan Heine: 165; Milne: 38-9, 70-71; Frank Nolting: 6, 9, 179, 187 (bottom left), 190; Jim Raftery: 99, 113; Pat Roberts: 139, 158, 159; Gisela Schregle: 211; Lavoy Sheppard: 207; J. Sorby: 108; Frank Sorge Fotograph: 189; Claus-Jörg Tuchel: 181; Dr Van Snow: 147; Lee Walsh: 25; John Weister: 120-21

FOR FURTHER INFORMATION
(Other than Canada and the USA)

My goal is to leave the world a better place, for horses
and people, than I found it. In that effort I invite you
to contact us on

Tel: 001 805 688 4382
E-mail: admin@MontyRoberts.com
www.montyroberts.com

for further information regarding clinics, conferences,
educational videos and other educational material,
including my four previously published books:

The Man Who Listens to Horses
Shy Boy: The Horse That Came in From the Wild
Horse Sense for People
From My Hands to Yours